Writing for Cash

Writing for Cash

What to write,
how to write,
where to sell it

JON ATKINSON and
BERYL SANDWELL

The Writing School, London

© Jon Atkinson and Beryl Sandwell 1975

Published in Great Britain by
The Writing School, Dundas House, 135 Notting Hill Gate,
London W11 3LB

ISBN 0 906486 00 9

Printed in Great Britain by
Billing & Sons Limited, Guildford, London and Worcester

Contents

Introduction   7

1 Tools for the Job   9

2 Writing the Short Filler Item   13
Finding subjects for fillers
Markets for fillers

3 Readers' Letters   19
First reply
Second reply
Choosing the right viewpoint
Children's letters
Keeping a record
Letters on a set subject
Seasonal letters
Markets for readers' letters

4 Gossip Column Writing   33
Finding suitable items
Examples of gossip-column writing

5 Writing for the Trade Press   41
Finding material for the trade press
Contacting the trade press
The American trade press
Some trade-press markets

6 Writing for the Women's Page   53
Subjects for the women's page
Examples of women's page articles

7 Writing for the Radio 65
Tips on writing a radio talk or story
Reading your script
Example of a radio talk

8 Women's Magazine Stories 77
Producing what the editor wants
Ingredients of a saleable story
Where to find plots
Characterisation
Dialogue
Emotion
Suspense
Reader identification
Endings
Markets for women's magazine stories
Example of a story

9 Writing the Confession Story 103
Confession-story formula
Markets for confession stories

10 Writing about your Hobby 117
General tips on writing about your hobby
Some magazines catering for hobbies
Sports writing
Letters on your favourite sport
Examples of articles

11 Writing Competition Slogans 131
Organising yourself to compete
Writing a slogan

In Conclusion 136

Index 139

Introduction

'Put it before them briefly, so they will read it, clearly, so they will appreciate it, picturesquely, so they will remember it and, above all, accurately, so they will be guided by its light.'

Joseph Pulitzer's advice to writers

This is a book about writing for money, something that can be achieved by people of any age, education or background. We hope it will interest those of you who have never tried, and encourage those who have tried and failed. It is for those of you who have always cherished a secret yearning to see your name in print, as well as others who are merely seeking a way of increasing their income. We hope some of our own enthusiasm for the craft of writing will rub off on you and that you too will derive immense satisfaction, pleasure and profit from it.

Writing is a fascinating pastime; it can also be a worthwhile career and a profitable spare-time occupation. We believe that anybody can earn money from writing. This is not wishful thinking on our part. It is something we have been doing for years. The secret for success lies in knowing exactly what to write, how to write and present it, and where to sell your work when it is done. In this book we suggest some of the ways to earn cash from your writing, though there are many more. The contents of the various chapters are based upon our own experience as freelance writers. We believe that what works for us will work for others too.

As in any other activity, the most useful guidance and information regarding the craft of writing can be given by those who have experienced success. The successful writer does not waste his talents and time producing work that stands little hope of acceptance. There are literally thousands of markets in this country and abroad, some almost unknown to the general public, where editors are crying out for material, and are willing to pay highly for what they want. We hope this book will show you where to find these markets, and how to ensure that you can produce work they will be delighted to buy.

We also hope our book will be the spark that fires your enthusiasm, the encouragement that keeps you persevering until you achieve success. Good luck and good writing.

1—Tools for the Job

All you need to become a writer is a notebook, pen or pencil, paper and a typewriter. You may think that the typewriter is an unnecessary expense when you first start to write, but actually it is an investment. Many editors will not consider accepting work that is not neatly typed and presented, and it is not necessary to buy a new or expensive machine. Typewriter shops often have good, second-hand models, which can be purchased at a fraction of the price of a new one. Alternatively, keep your eye on the advertisement column in your local newspaper, and you may be lucky enough to pick up a bargain. Unless you have room for a standard-sized typewriter, buy one of the smaller portables; these weigh just a few pounds and can be quickly and easily moved around when required. If you have had no training in the use of a typewriter, a course of typing lessons would help you to produce neat, professional looking work. Most Colleges of Further Education include typing courses in their curricula.

For a writer, notebooks are essential; have them scattered around the house; one by your bedside, another in the kitchen and one in every handbag or jacket pocket. Don't try to make do with one, because it will always be missing when you have your best ideas. Once you get started on the writing game, you will be amazed how often you take out your notebook to jot down quotes, anecdotes, amusing and serious ideas that constantly float into your mind. You will discover, too, that unless you immediately make a note of that marvellous bit of conversation you heard when your children were on their own, it will be forgotten by the end of the day.

Keep your notebook small enough to fit into the palm of your hand. People sometimes become a little scared when they see you scribbling in a large notebook. It looks official and therefore frightening.

You can never have too many pens and pencils scattered around the house. There is nothing so infuriating as having to hunt for pen and pad when you suddenly think up a marvellous idea.

Typing paper can be bought by the ream from any stationer; the size to use is A4. Choose a paper that is neither too flimsy nor too thick.

Having collected together your tools, you are all set to start writing for cash. Here are a few tips to help you earn that first cheque:

1. If your spelling is weak, keep a dictionary at your elbow and use it.
2. Never use a long sentence if a short one will do.
3. Be as neat as possible in the presentation of your work.
4. Always use double spacing and allow $1\frac{1}{2}$-inch margins down each side of your paper. Break up your work into paragraphs and indent five spaces on your typewriter at the beginning of each new paragraph. Don't try to save paper by squashing in an extra line right at the bottom of a page.
5. Remember that editors are busy people and their eyesight is valuable, so don't send grubby, difficult to decipher typing.
6. Number each page clearly at the top, and on each

succeeding page after the first, put the title on the top and your name and town, just in case the sheets become detached. When sending more than one page of copy to a newspaper office, at the bottom right hand corner of each page type the letters 'mf' (more follows) to warn the editor there is more to follow. On the last page type the word 'ends'.

7. Put your full name and address in the top right-hand corner of the first sheet and repeat this again at the bottom of the last sheet.

8. Clip your sheets firmly together at the top left-hand corner using a paper clip and never a pin.

9. Always include a stamped addressed envelope if you want your material to be returned to you. Short items, such as readers' letters and fillers, are not returned, so a self-addressed envelope need not be enclosed.

10. Don't write to an editor asking why he has rejected your article or story. Try again.

11. Keep a record book showing details of every item you write and send out.

12. A simple filing system may be introduced as you progress with your work.

13. Earnings from freelance writing are subject to Income Tax, and if you are worried about your tax liability, you should get in touch with your local Income Tax Officer.

Every writer builds up a small library of books of reference. Begin with a good dictionary—the *Concise Oxford Dictionary*—and add *Roget's Thesaurus:* Chambers' *Biographical Dictionary:* Everyman's *Dictionary of Quotations and Proverbs,* and Brewer's *Dictionary of Phrase and Fable.* These will start you off, and no doubt you will want to add to this collection as you branch out as a writer.

A monthly publication called the Contributors' Bulletin will give you a great deal of helpful advice, as well as keeping you up to date with current market requirements. Any beginner will find a subscription to this is money well spent, for it is a mine of fascinating and useful information.

Being a writer means that you must inevitably spend much of your time working alone at your typewriter. In most towns you will find a local Writers' Circle or Club where you can meet fellow writers to discuss problems and obtain help and advice. Call in at your local library for information regarding your nearest Writers' Circle and pop along to their next meeting.

2—Writing the Short Filler Item

Jon Atkinson

Every editor is constantly looking for entertaining, interesting, instructive and amusing little pieces to fill up the small spaces left at the bottom of a page when articles or news stories end. This is where the wide awake freelance writer can earn money by supplying editors with jokes, anecdotes, recipes, hints, and in fact, any up-to-a-hundred-word item which will interest magazine and newspaper readers.

The beauty of filler items is that you can write them down as you see, hear or think of them, when travelling by car, bus or train, peeling the spuds or making the beds. Keep your ears constantly cocked for the unusual and interesting gossip which in itself can become a filler. I'll deal with material suitable for gossip columns in a separate chapter.

Finding subjects for fillers

In the office where I work, we have soccer and rugby teams which play every week in the winter. Usually nothing that is newsworthy happens, but recently they won a trophy. The filler item which resulted from this win read as follows:

The toast at the bar was 'bottoms up' after a Newcastle office rugby team won a seven-a-side Ordsall Trophy recently under floodlights at Mill Lane, York.

Sides from York, Leeds and Retford took part, and the Newcastle side did not concede a point in defeating Leeds 27-0 and Retford 4-0 in the final.

The trophy, a brown wooden toilet seat bearing the inscription on the sit-upon-side 'Seven-a-side tournament ... Ordsall Trophy' was presented to the Newcastle captain. The Retford staff had salvaged the seat from a derelict building.

Another day, travelling on a bus over the familiar route to the office, I kept my eye looking for changes and the unusual, and spotted a notice on a scrapyard door, to give me this short saleable filler: 'Beware Large Dog. Survivors will be prosecuted!'

Listen to the chatter of children who frequently come out with sayings both wise and witty. Women's magazines use such sayings to fill up column gaps at the end of articles and short stories.

Watch out for the helpful, usual and unusual solutions to everyday problems. Get them all down in your notebook, before you forget, so that you can write them up later at your leisure. You can even earn extra cash at work too, by thinking up ways to improve production, or save the firm's time and money. If you get a good idea, put it in writing and hand it in to the management. Most firms these days pay well for bright ideas. Friends of mine have enjoyed family holidays, and won television sets, radios and money for their profitable brainwaves.

As a housewife, have you found a new way of tackling one of the many mundane jobs you carry out each week? If you are brilliant, you may have a hundred such tips, and each one can earn money for you if you write them up and sell them as fillers.

What about the time you put your foot through the

bedroom ceiling, trying to catch a bird in the loft? Any funny happening in your household, which may not have seemed so funny when it happened, can be written up as an amusing filler in an informal, conversational style and offered to an editor.

Type your fillers on A4 paper, keeping a carbon copy for your own reference which may be filed in a cardboard envelope file used only for fillers.

Put your name clearly in the top right-hand corner of the paper, and give each filler item a number which should be in the top left-hand corner. Keep a record in a small notebook of each number and filler so that at any time you will be able to check which editors have received these items from you. You can send any number of fillers to an editor at the one time. I usually send any number up to six. No stamped addressed envelope is needed for their return if not used. If you have received no payment for a particular filler after an editor has had it for six months, you can safely assume he does not intend to use the item and you can offer it elsewhere.

If you are not sure whether your filler is suitable, ask yourself the following questions before sending it off to a newspaper or magazine:

1. Is it a solution to a problem which the readers of the paper will encounter?
2. Will it be helpful or seem funny to those readers?
3. If sending a recipe, will it be tasty, nutritious, easy and cheap to prepare?
4. Have all the ingredients, weights, times and ins-tructions been checked?

Keep your eye open for printing errors in the press, as these make excellent fillers. Cut them out together with the paragraph before the howler and the one after. Paste onto a postcard along with the title of the paper in which it appeared, the date of the edition and send it to *Competitors' Journal, Weekend* or *She,* who pay for each howler they print.

Editors not only in this country but all over the world are always on the look out for new sources of supply to keep a freshness and variety before their readers. Find the names and addresses of newspapers and magazines in the *Writers' and Artists' Year Book* and *Willing's Press Guide.* (Incidentally, we have omitted the addresses of all publications mentioned in this book as they may be out of date by the time you come to read it. Look them up in *Willing's.*)

Remember that almost everything we do in life, anything that happens to us can, with a little ingenuity and thought, be turned into saleable filler material.

Not only are daily, weekly and monthly newspapers and magazines interested in filler items, but many of the hundreds of trade and house magazines are fruitful markets for items slanted to their particular needs.

Markets for fillers
How do we set about finding markets for fillers? I buy at least one different periodical each week. I go through it very carefully, noting in particular the advertisements, for they are your guide to the people who buy the paper. I note the slant and style of the articles, news stories and fillers, and the whole make-up of the magazine. I look at the length of the sentences and paragraphs so that I will be able to supply copy, including fillers, which will be tailor-made for that particular magazine, and consequently stand a better chance of being bought by that market. As in all branches of writing, market study pays dividends and increases your chances of selling successfully.

Write about the things, peoples and places that you

know intimately, not forgetting to note the witty and humorous sayings of friends and foes, for potential use as fillers. Do you know any unusual party games? Or gardening hints? Are you good at making things? Don't forget it helps to send neat simple drawings showing dimensions and materials used; if you can't draw, send a photograph.

Many periodicals pay for short criticisms of television programmes. The daily *Sun* and *Sunday Mirror* are examples. Weekly magazines such as *Weekend*, *Weekly News*, *Saturday Titbits*, and *Sunday Mail* as well as many provincial weeklies are good markets for fillers.

One world-wide magazine, the *Reader's Digest,* is always on the search for fillers, so much so, that apart from the end-of-article fillers and other anecdotal items, they have special pages for 'Humour in Uniform', which must be true, unpublished stories based on the experiences of men and women in uniform. Another page of fillers called 'Life's like That' features true, unpublished stories from your own experience, which reveal human nature and at the same time provide appealing and humorous sidelights on everyday life in Britain.

There is a 'College Rag' page which prints your own funny stories about life at college or university. The *Reader's Digest* always requires fillers for its regular features each month, viz: 'Points to Ponder', 'Personal Glimpses', 'Laughter: the Best Medicine', and 'Towards more Picturesque Speech'.

Your payment for published items in the *Reader's Digest* can be any amount from £10 to £50, according to length and the editor's evaluation. It will pay you to buy a copy of the *Reader's Digest* the next time you visit a book-stall, to study the pages and columns I have mentioned.

If you really strip every magazine and newspaper with your eyes, you may find the filler space that you can quite easily fill. With a little thought and three hundred words or less you should come up with something to suit the editor which will bring you your just reward ... a cheque!

3—Readers' Letters

Jon Atkinson

Most of us have felt the urge to write to the press at some time in our lives, probably when we feel strongly about some current topic or injustice. Sometimes, in the frenzy of the moment, the letter may get written; more often than not it ends up in the waste-paper basket instead of on the editor's desk. The next time you get the urge to speak your mind on paper, why not aim it at the readers' letter page of a newspaper or magazine?

Many publications pay cash for printed letters; this amount may be quite modest in some cases, perhaps £1 or £2 for a letter from a dozen to a hundred words in length. Some magazines pay considerably more while others offer useful prizes instead of cash ranging from tea-sets to fountain pens.

It seems to be a very human failing to want to air our views and display our knowledge in print, and we read with interest and pleasure the correspondence column in our daily newspaper or weekly magazine. The markets for readers' letters are many, and several publications contain whole pages made up entirely of contributions received from their readers. This is an all-the-year-round opening, and one of the easiest ways to start writing for cash.

The first essential step to take when starting to send letters to the press, is to find out which publications publish and pay for contributions printed on their letter page. Normally the ones which do pay state so quite plainly at the end of the letter page. Make a list of the paying markets. You will be surprised how many there are. Besides the daily newspapers, most of the women's magazines and specialist magazines contain a regular readers' letter spot.

Be on the look out for unusual publications and whenever you have the opportunity to glance through an unfamiliar periodical, look out for a readers' letter page. Browsing through the piles of old magazines at the hairdresser or dentist may unearth another market. Do not make the mistake of thinking that all printed letters are alike, and that what will suit one magazine will automatically be acceptable to another. Before sending your letter off, check the length, style and treatment of letters published in the newspaper of your choice. These will provide your guidelines.

What can you write about that will make a successful reader's letter? How do you get your ideas? How do you set them down? Almost everything that happens to you in your daily life can be a source of letter ideas; everyday incidents, humdrum or unusual, may be written up entertainingly in such a way as to cause interest and response.

Use your eyes and keep you ears open. Listen to the things people say. Be inquisitive when something new crops up. Your opinion of the latest labour-saving gadget after first-hand experience of its use, will stand a good chance of publication. Readers' letters giving information are always popular, so make use of the knowledge you have acquired and let it earn cash for you. Garden hints, new uses for used envelopes or old razor blades, practical guidance for home decorators, recipes for home-made wines and your special cure for tired feet may provide entertaining reading.

Several newspapers and magazines that run regular letter pages will sometimes pose a question at the bottom of the column, requesting readers to send in their answers. The daily newspaper the *Sun* and the Sunday newspaper *News of the World* do this frequently. On one occasion the *News of the World* posed the question: 'What was the kindly act you regretted?' The reply I promptly wrote and despatched read: 'I felt sorry for a workman and invited him into my house for a cup of tea and a sandwich. He was so grateful, he helped himself to my watch!'

The £2.50 I received I put towards a new watch. The incident had happened some time before and had been recorded in a notebook and reading the *News of the World* question brought it back to mind. Remember to use your notebook regularly to jot down any incident that can be turned into an interesting letter.

Editors usually welcome letters dealing with current controversial subjects. During a period of severe drought when people were being warned not to use hosepipes on the garden and entreated to conserve water in the home whenever possible, the following paragraph appeared in the sports section of a provincial newspaper. '. . . Kempton, where the £40,000 Benson and Hedges sponsored Eclipse Stakes will be run on Saturday, has been watered for the past three weeks. . . .' Feeling infuriated about this apparent waste of water, I sent a letter expressing my protest to the *News of the World* and let my anger earn £2.50 for me.

Any everyday occurrence may spark off an idea for a reader's letter. Here is one example: 'A friend called to borrow my garden barrow a year ago to take some rubbish to the tip. I have not seen my friend or the barrow since.' Or: 'By what clues do you judge character?' This question in a newspaper brought in a flood of replies, each of which earned £1 for its writer including one which read: 'I watch people's hands. The nervous don't know where to put them. They constantly fidget. The easily agitated types hold their hands tightly or grip hold of something, whilst those who are quietly calm let their hands rest limply.'

Children are always a rich source of material for letters. Their sayings, quaint or embarrassing, when related by adults, are found frequently in the letter pages of women's magazines. Here is an example of a prize-winning letter:

> The Women's Lib movement is getting supporters at an early age, judging from the experience in our household. Last night when my small daughter said her prayers, she ended with 'Ah women!' instead of 'Amen'!
>
> 'I'm tired of saying "Amen",' she explained. 'Why shouldn't I think of women for a change?'

Housewives find that their grumbles and grievances over trivial domestic matters can be turned into cheques from letter-page editors, particularly when new information or personal experiences are included. Homely, everyday objects can provide the subject-matter, such as the daily bottle of milk which inspired the following comment:

> It always amazes me that householders leave bottles of milk on the doorstep for hours even when they are at home and could easily grab the bottles and put them into the fridge. Quite apart from the fact that the bottles may be stolen, the householders are in fact being robbed of goodness, for exposure to sunlight for lengthy periods causes milk to lose vitamin B (riboflavin).

The subject of the following letter published in *My Weekly* earned its contributor publication on the letter page and a cheque:

Like most housewives I am grateful for any help in the home from my husband. He is very good at washing the dishes, but he doesn't seem able to wring out the dishcloth properly. When he's finished the job, there's always a soggy mess of a dishcloth oozing in a pool of water, left on my work surface by the sink. Then from the next room I usually hear the ominous dripping sound as the water forms a puddle on my nice clean floor! I have often shown him how to wring out a cloth, but he hasn't cottoned on yet and we've been married seventeen years. My friend next door says her husband is just the same. Isn't it amazing how men can hold down a responsible job for years and yet can't do a simple thing like that?

Women's magazine letter pages are good markets for comments on family life. If you read a wide selection of printed letters you may have an idea for a follow-up letter on the same subject, which may catch the editor's interest.

Be as original as you can, remembering that some hundreds of readers' letters are received daily. To be chosen for publication yours must stand out from the rest. Write and re-write your letter until it contains all you want to say using the fewest number of words. Put your points clearly and briefly; if you include facts, remember to check that you have got them right. Many periodicals ask contributors to their letter pages to submit postcards only, and even when this is not requested, it is a good idea and acceptable to most editors. Fitting your words into the restricted space available on an ordinary postcard is a good way of learning to express yourself concisely.

Never submit the same letter to several publications at the same time. However if, after a reasonable time, your letter has not appeared on the letter page, you may send your letter elsewhere. The usual time to wait varies with the publication concerned; some editors may use a letter after holding it for several months. A general guide is as follows: for the letter page in a monthly magazine, wait six months; in a weekly, three months; and in a daily newspaper, six weeks.

There are no specific rates which apply to letters in general. Payment varies according to the magazine or newspaper which publishes your letter, and is generally received during the month following publication. Occasionally there is a 'star letter' spot. If you achieve this, your cheque may be five times the normal amount paid for readers' letters.

On reading a number of published letters, you may be surprised by their brevity. As a beginner, you may find it hard to know what to cut out without spoiling your story. Here is an example of a badly written letter followed by a polished, pruned version that achieved publication.

'Have you ever had an unexpected windfall?' This question was posed by a daily newspaper.

First reply
'I was out shopping one Saturday afternoon, hoping to buy some shoes when my friend said: "My! Isn't it a blustery day?" . . . as I turned to chase my hat along the main road. We both walked with our heads down as the dust cluttered our eyeballs. Pieces of paper stuck to our clothes as we battled on. Suddenly I saw a green piece of paper floating by and thought it was a soup label. It

24

settled at my feet for a split second as the wind gasped for breath. My friend said: "Look, there's a pound note under your foot." "Don't be daft," I said. "Money doesn't come that easy!" My eyes nearly popped out when I looked and saw that she was right. It was a "oncer". My friend and I decided that instead of splitting it fifty-fifty, we would buy a premium bond and if there were any winnings we would share the proceeds. We checked the bond prize lists each month, not knowing then that three months would have to elapse before our bond was included in its first draw. Surprise! Surprise! In its first draw, I received a cheque for £50.'

Second well-written, brief, money-spinning reply
'On a blustery day in the city, the wind blew a £1 note right to my feet. I picked it up, bought a Premium Bond with it, and won £50 three months later.'

From the above examples, you will see that the second story version has far more impact. Prune your sentences hard until you cannot cut out another word. Taken-from-life anecdotes, presented in the form of a reader's letter, can be as brief as you like. The use of dialogue often cuts out unnecessary words, while making your letter more interesting to read. Here is an example: 'Having been sent to tell his Gran that breakfast was ready, my young son, a keen horseman, announced: "She's coming. She's just putting her saddle on!"'

To make sure that your contribution is of a similar length to those already published in your chosen letter page market, count each word. Make sure your letter is no longer than any the editor has chosen to print.

Having written and despatched your letter to your letter page market, it is only human to want to know that it has been received at the other end, and not lost in the post. It is impossible, however, to be sure of receiving an acknowledgement. Some publications always send a printed form intimating that the letter has been received. Others do not. Often your first hint of success is the sight of your letter in print or an envelope containing a cheque.

When cutting down your words to a minimum on your postcard, do not forget to include your own name and address. It is not necessary to enclose a stamped addressed envelope for the return of readers' letters, as it is not editorial practice to do this. It is as well to remember that editors do not use material, however excellently written, when the writer has failed to enclose his name and address. This may never appear in print and indeed rarely does on a readers' letter page where space is scarce. Mrs A. V., Nottingham, may be the only clue to the identity of the writer of a particular letter.

Choosing the right viewpoint
When studying your readers' letters markets, find out whether the editor prefers the male or female viewpoint. The majority of published letters in a women's magazine may be written from a woman's angle, but will also include contributions from men. As there are many letter markets available in the pages of most of the women's magazines, the female viewpoint may prove to be more profitable. As a writer, whether male or female, you should choose and write your letter from the angle favoured by the editor.

When first starting to send off readers' letters, it may seem difficult to think up suitable ideas, but after some practice you will find that each day incidents happen which can, with a little thought, be turned into letter page submissions. Don't let them slip out of your memory before you have time to write them up. Use your notebook to record the idea. It need only be a couple of words or a few scribbled sentences, but it will be enough to jog your memory and bring the incident back to mind later, when there is time to give it some thought.

Although editors may pay small amounts for published letters, these can soon add up to a considerable total if you make a habit of sending off your postcards. There are writers who earn regular incomes from this type of writing alone. The secret of their success is that they set themselves a readers' letter target and keep to it. One letter writer tells me he tries to send off one letter each day, 365 a year, and although not every one achieves publication, he earns £150 or more a year from this type of writing alone.

Another letter writer aims to pay for major household bills from his proceeds, and a woman letter-writer has recarpeted the whole of her home from her readers' letter cheques.

Children's letters
It is never too soon to get the daily readers' letter habit, and there are opportunities for children's letters in the juvenile magazines and children's pages of adult publications. Young people these days are quick to comment on current topics that touch their lives. Your children may have firm ideas on controversial subjects like school discipline, the length of holidays, horror films or community projects. If so, encourage them to put their thoughts into words. Instead of cheques, children usually receive suitable gifts for their contributions. The first thing you ever have published is always the most memorable for a child or an adult, an occasion never to be forgotten even if the writer goes on

27

to produce a bestseller afterwards. My own writing career was launched at the age of twelve when I wrote a letter to the children's page of the Newcastle *Sunday Sun* and subsequently saw my masterpiece in print. I could never bring myself to use the large coloured crayons which were my first reward from writing, but they have been worn down to stumps by my own children, and have been used by them to win dozens of colouring competitions.

Keeping a record of letters submitted

Once you discover that you are able to keep up a regular output of readers' letters, the use of a record book is essential. In a notebook, under the following headings, write details of every letter you despatch. This will help you to avoid duplication.

1. Date of submission
2. Subject-matter
3. Number of words
4. Where sent
5. Accepted
6. Date of payment

Very little time is required to keep this form of record up-to-date, and an occasional glance at it will show you when a particular letter has not been accepted. If a reasonable time has lapsed since its despatch, you may re-write and submit to another market.

Letters on a set subject

In order to encourage a flow of letters, from time to time, an editor will ask for letters on a particular subject. A daily newspaper asked its readers to write about the tyrant or good fairy in the family circle. A money-spinning reply was as follows:

The tyrants in our household are the ever-indulgent

aunts. They buy our children everything they want, and take their side in family arguments. The good fairy is my mother who is always ready to cool heated situations and placate the vanquished in arguments. She even backs us in important questions such as decisions about the children's future, even though she sometimes thinks that we are in the wrong.

Seasonal letters

Problems encountered at special seasons of the year make interesting topics for a letter page. One Christmas, the following appeared in a local newspaper and is a good example of the type of letter an editor might pay for and publish in December.

Christmas is still four weeks away but already shoals of Christmas cards, seals, etc., have been sent to householders on behalf of various charities. In our house, we have received by post three dozen Christmas cards from different charities asking us to send 50p for twelve cards by return of post.

I am neither mean nor uncharitable, but I think that the posting of unsolicited charity cards and seals to households is a piece of sharp practice. The senders are playing on the kindness and generosity of the recipients. If you don't want them you think: 'It's a good cause and it will look bad if I send them back.'

Many of these cards are sent to pensioners who cannot afford to send the cards back, and rarely is a pre-paid label enclosed with the cards. Usually the pensioner pays for the return postage and cuts down on some necessity to cover the cost. It is time charitable organisations took steps to stop this racket.

When submitting a seasonal letter, it is as well to

29

remember that many publications go to press some time ahead of publication date. Send off your letter in good time, so that it may be considered for inclusion in the appropriate issue.

Although a well-written, original letter on almost any subject will stand a good chance of achieving publication, it is as well to avoid certain topics which may give offence to a reader. Every editor will have his own ideas as to what can and cannot appear in his publication. You may discover some of these by trial and error, but as a general policy, a letter-writer would be wise to avoid unfavourable reference to proprietary brands of goods, and comments on religious beliefs or racial matters. If you are doubtful about the acceptability of any subject, avoid it. Let ordinary good taste decide for you what not to mention.

If you are a beginner in the readers' letter field, you may rack your brain for ideas and forget your own special interest. If you are keen on cars or caterpillars or cleanliness in restaurants, you will have, at your finger tips, the material for innumerable readers' letters. Use the letter page of your favourite hobby magazine to ask a question or give a helpful tip.

Markets for readers' letters

A comprehensive list of all publications that feature a letter page would be very long, and undoubtedly out-of-date before it could be printed. There are some newspapers and magazines that have been running a regular readers' letter page for years, and others that include them from time to time.

By your own vigilance and constant search for markets, you will keep unearthing new ones. This is a changing market, but the rewards are there for anyone prepared to keep an eye on it. Each time you spot a letter page in a magazine you had not known existed, you increase your chances of success

The list given here is intended as a guide to start you looking for your own letter markets. The addresses are not included, as they may change. No overseas publications are included, but there are obviously many of these where letters may be sent. Addresses of British publications and names and addresses of overseas publications can be found in the *Writers' and Artists' Year Book.* A specimen copy will usually be sent on request. Overseas newspapers are listed in *Willing's Press Guide.*

Woman
Woman's Realm
Woman's Own
News of the World
Hers
Loving
She
Sun
My Weekly
People's Friend
Competitors' Journal
Sunday Sun
Saturday Titbits

Weekend
Sunday People
Family Circle
Living
Good Housekeeping
Ideal Home
Sunday Mail
Sunday Post
Sunday Mirror
Annabel
Red Letter
True Story

4—Gossip Column Writing

Jon Atkinson

Nearly every local newspaper you pick up carries a gossip page. This is made up of short paragraphs and pictures about people and places with a local slant or interest. We are all curious to learn what is happening in our particular part of the country, especially when the information is entertainingly presented. Let's be honest, men as well as women enjoy a gossip, which is why the gossip pages in our newspapers are well read and very popular with readers.

It is usually the job of one journalist on the staff of a newspaper to compile and edit the gossip page. This often has a permanent title such as 'Mersey Echoes', 'Out and About' or 'Chatterbox'. No doubt you always turn with interest to read the gossip page of your local newspaper, knowing it keeps you up-to-date with news of local personalities and their doings. The gossip page in a daily newspaper has a wider readership. When you realise that it appears regularly each day, six days a week throughout the year, you become aware of the large amount of varied and interesting copy required to fill the gossip page. And whilst the journalist whose job it is to run the page is helped considerably by his colleagues on the paper, he is always looking out for good copy sent in by the freelance writer. Here is an opening which you may be able to fill. If you can help to provide variety for this day-to-day column, you will be paid well for your efforts.

Finding suitable items

Finding suitable items for the gossip page is often a matter of luck, plus the ability to recognise gossip column material when you see it. When you first start to read the gossip columns with a view to studying their contents and aiming to send in suitable material, you may feel that you could never produce anything worth printing in the column. Nothing fascinating ever happens to you, you may think, and all the people you know are too ordinary to be interesting. Among your friends and acquaintances there is no one who has sailed single-handed round the Horn or taken off in a hot-air balloon.

Don't despair, for a careful, detailed study of the gossip columns will convince you that the interesting bits which are read so avidly are usually about the ordinary man-in-the-street and his wife. The appeal here seems to be that we turn to the gossip column to read about people like ourselves and their happenings. Perhaps we enjoy hearing that, just like us, other people have their share of delights and disasters. It is not necessary to live a gay social life, mix with glamorous people, or attend important functions in your search for gossip-page material. What you have to acquire is the ability to write about ordinary people and situations in an entertaining easily read style. Try to remember that readers of the gossip page are looking for human interest and drama as well as information, and therefore the writer must present his material to them in an appealing form. A light-hearted, chatty style and the ability to amuse are invaluable assets to the gossip writer.

When you first begin to write, it may be difficult for you to make up your mind whether the anecdote you are about to put down on paper will end up as an article for the women's page, a paragraph in a trade journal or a piece in your local gossip column. The truth is that it could easily suit all three, and indeed be written up in three different ways to earn three cheques for you. Unfortunately there is no magic set of rules laid down for you to follow in order to sell one story three times over. The only way to learn how to make the most of the material that comes your way is to read and re-read the women's pages, trade journals and gossip columns until it becomes apparent to you how each editor presents information to the reader. You will be astonished how the constant reading of any periodical or column gives you the feel of the publication. One editor may go for crisp, businesslike sentences; another may prefer a more leisurely, humorous pace. These differences will show themselves after a little study, so that in the end it becomes second nature to write up your stuff in a way you know will appeal to the editor.

Examples of gossip-column writing

Although the basic story behind your thrice-selling idea is one and the same, this does not mean that you have merely to copy it out three times and send off to three markets. Each editor wants a different slant and style to suit his readers, but this is something you will discover for yourself when doing your market study. To illustrate how an ordinary news item sent to a trade paper can be re-written and adapted for a local newspaper gossip column, I sent a short story on the installation of a new anti-theft device in a local store to a drapery trade paper. This was merely a report, giving the name and address of the shop and proprietor, amounting to no more than fifty words. The following piece on the same subject was subsequently published in the gossip column of the local evening newspaper:

35

According to recent newspaper reports, the battle against the ubiquitous shoplifter seems to be raged rather more determinedly in the south of the country than here in the north-east. But that is not to say that the experienced garment whipper has it all her own way in our local stores.

Quite complex new gadgets are coming into use in the fight against the thieves and they can take it from me that they'll have a sticky time if they decide to go on an illicit shopping spree in the new — fashion shop. Every garment on display there has a patented plastic tab attached to it and the tab can only be removed by an assistant putting it into a machine. Anyone foolish enough to steal a garment will soon discover the error of her ways. Alarms will sound and other gadgets activated by the tag will draw attention to the thief. Mrs —, the manageress, tells me she believes it is the first fashion shop in the city to be equipped with this anti-theft device.

One of the greatest assets a writer can possess is a keen observation and the ability to turn quite ordinary and unremarkable daily occurrences into saleable material. It is easy to become bored and unseeing when you catch the same train to work each morning, see the same faces along the same old street and return home each night along the familiar route. Do try to spot the unusual and unexpected. Train your eyes and ears so that they work for you every moment of the day. Even when your daily job is absorbing your attention, listen and look out for the relatively unimportant incidents that you can snap up and set down as gossip paragraphs. When a friend of mine returned from holiday and I asked him how he'd enjoyed himself, he enthused about the weather and the hotel and the food he'd eaten. His remarks were quite mundane until he mentioned his train journey back home. I made a mental note of all he said, and later wrote the following, which was published in the local evening newspaper:

When travelling daily to work by train I have always had a burning desire to pull the communication cord, but the thought of paying the £25 fine for the privilege has always deterred me. How I envy Mr Jimmy Brown, a railwayman, who pulled the communication cord on a recent journey and it cost him nothing at all.

Returning with his wife from a sun-drenched holiday in San Remo, he was on a fast continental express travelling at ninety miles an hour when things began to happen. 'We were between Toulon and Marseilles,' said Mr Brown, 'when my wife said she could smell something burning. Looking around the coach and in the corridors, I could find nothing, but when I glanced out of the window, I saw the train was on fire. I pulled the communication cord and the train ground to a stop. Passengers and railwaymen jumped down onto the track and fought the fire which was fortunately confined to a parcels van. It was detached from the train and 45 minutes later we were on our way home none the worse for our experience.'

As you can see, the above gossip material was really someone else's story, and once you are on the look out for this type of copy, you will be surprised to find how you can utilise other people's comments and conversation in this way. Reminiscences about the past pepper most people's remarks from time to time and these can often trigger off ideas for gossip paragraphs. One day a friend showed me an old letter from which came the following gossip item:

> Most of us grumble at some time about the hours we have to work and the rewards we get for the time we put in. And in the same breath, a lot of folk wax nostalgic about 'the good old days'. I have a feeling they'd change their song if they had to put up with the kind of situation which prompted a certain Mr D. Munro to write to his employers in August 1848. A friend has just shown me a facsimile of Mr Munro's cry from the heart written when he was stationmaster at Holytown in Scotland.
>
> 'I beg leave to bring before your notice the following remarks relative to my pay here and the duty I have to perform,' Mr Munro wrote. 'I have to sell all the tickets and make out all the returns. Secondly I have to keep the time of fifteen engines with the number of wagons to and from each place. Thirdly I have to attend to the goods that go from here and come by Caledonian Railways. My time on duty is from 6 am to 9 pm. I am paid at the same rate per week as the porter and the pointsman at the station, viz., eighteen shilling per week and some weeks my pay is reduced as low as thirteen shillings by losing on the tickets. It would put me under infinite obligations to you, Sir, if you would have the goodness to represent my case to those who can advance my pay according to my labour.'

Topical items in the news can bear fruit for the gossip writer. Or, when anything annoying or strange happens in your own home, work off the annoyance by writing up your moan. Then at least the payment received may assuage your irritation. It did for me when some idiot struck at our household one morning recently. In print it read as follows:

A practical joker in town is proving a menace to milkman and householders. Mrs — of — on opening her front door to collect her usual three pints of milk, found a note lying beside the bottles.

'Please leave twelve extra pints of milk,' the note said in blue ink and strange handwriting. It was signed, Mrs Nutta. Printed underneath was a message from the milkman who had already called: 'Have not that much extra. Will call back later.'

Later, the milkman arrived carrying the 12 extra bottles of milk. Only then did he realise that he had been the victim of a practical joke.

I hope these examples will help you to realise that gossip-page material is all around you, every day of your life, and that this is one branch of writing that is wide open for anyone who chooses it. Hours of research and specialised knowledge are not necessary. A lively interest in your fellow man and the world around you will pay dividends. To be a successful writer, you must train yourself to be observant at all times, not a difficult task. After a short while it becomes a habit and you will find yourself taking great delight in turning your daily crop of simple observations into valuable cheques. Make a start by sending gossip items to your local morning or evening newspaper. Once you have tasted success you will agree that this is a fascinating branch of writing, bringing something new and interesting into your life at every turn.

5—Writing for the Trade Press

Jon Atkinson

When we speak of journalism most of us think of the national daily and evening newspapers, the local papers and the magazine press. If we think only of these, we miss a very important outlet for our work; the trade press is a highly responsible literary market which can provide the ideal opening for those hoping to break into journalism.

Hundreds of trade papers exist in the British Isles and in the United States of America there are over two thousand trade publications. Every industry and profession has its own specialised journal: butchers, bakers, engineers, drapers, nurses and even under-takers—all have their own paper dealing with their particular trade or vocation. Weekly and monthly trade papers such as these are always hungry for news, and a large proportion of their news intelligence is bought from freelance contributors, for in most instances the staff employed by the trade journal is small. For the hopeful freelance, here is an opportunity to write for cash.

Wherever you live, in town or village, you will be among people quietly carrying on their day-to-day jobs in shops, offices and factories. The trade press is interested in supplying its readers with the latest in-formation it can glean on any particular industry or profession, and if you can supply editors with interesting and up-to-date facts or news items, then nine times out of ten, they will buy it from you. Like all copy it must be new, interesting and entertaining factual stuff. The editors want to hear of happenings connected with their trade which will make absorbing reading for their readers who are in the same line of business.

If you are looking for a way to augment your annual income, writing for the trade press can prove highly profitable. Most trade publications have been in existence for many years. They have an assured income from people in the trade who order the magazine by subscription, and pay for it annually, so that a trade paper editor has a very good idea what money will be available throughout the year to run his publication. In this way trade papers differ from ordinary magazines that are displayed on bookstalls in the hope that the public will buy them.

Trade-paper editors are invariably most helpful. They publish quickly and pay promptly. Many writers who are busy working on novels or other literary work find that it pays them to produce copy for the trade press and thereby earn some cash while the longer work is being written.

Finding material for the trade press
Although when you first give a thought to trade press writing, you wonder what will interest an editor, in time and with a little practice, you will develop a 'nose' for trade news. You learn to follow up odd items of news that come to your ears in conversation or appear in your local newspapers. A two-line report tucked away at the bottom of a page may provide you with the basic information required to write several interesting pieces for trade magazines.

Always check the facts before you begin. This is easily

done by ringing up the directors, managers and staff of firms. You will find, after making a few enquiries, that you will have at your fingertips the information to write a bigger, better story than you ever thought possible after reading that two-line report in the local newspaper.

I have always found that the editors and staff working on trade papers are unfailingly courteous in their dealings with the freelance contributor. During a recent emergency, I sent some copy to a trade paper, but by the time it arrived in their office, the emergency was over and the copy was useless in the form in which it had been written. In a normally busy newspaper office, my piece would have ended up on the 'spike', a stake attached to a weight on which the editorial staff deposit all unsuitable copy received. Not so in the trade paper office. My copy was returned to me along with a charming letter from the diary editor which read: 'You might like to re-submit this story as a general gossip item since it is too late now to run reference to the emergency.'

Admittedly this is a small matter, but it illustrates the close bond that is built up between most trade-paper editorial staff and the contributor. And such a nice gesture gives the writer the urge to dig out more copy for that particular journal.

Don't imagine that a trade paper will print badly written, poorly researched material. Trade magazines cater for the specialist and are formulated with as much care and expense as are the larger circulation magazines such as *She* or *Woman*.

Contacting the trade press
Although there are such a large number of trade papers in existence, many of them are known only to the trade

concerned. It is, however, an easy matter to discover the names and addresses of all the trade journals as these are listed in the *Willing's Press Guide* and the *Writers' and Artists' Year Book,* which, if you don't own them, should be available in the reference section of your local library. As a beginner you must browse through the lists and pick out several trade papers which appeal to you and for which you think you could write.

First, write to each of your chosen trade-paper editors, expressing your interest in supplying material and asking for a specimen copy of their journals so that you can study style and format. Remember to enclose a large, stamped addressed envelope and you will find that most editors will oblige.

This first contact is most important to the would-be trade-press writer. The editor may already have a correspondent in your area, supplying him with all the local information he requires, and if this is so, you will not waste further time on that particular paper. If, however, he is eager to contact a correspondent in your district, he will send you, by return, a news correspondents' general information sheet.

This general information sheet will give the journal's telephone number, the day it is published, the editor's name and other relevant details. The news editor's name and telephone extension are always useful in case you need to contact him for information. The telephone extension number of the copytaker is the one you will need to know when you have urgent news which may go into the next issue of the trade paper. The procedure when you telephone in your urgent copy is as follows:
1. Give the copytaker your name and full address.
2. Dictate your copy, spelling out names and places to avoid mistakes.
3. When the piece is finished, ask the copytaker if he

has any queries regarding correct spelling, dates, etc.

The general information sheet will also give you the main news interests, explaining what the editor requires in the way of copy. This includes any topic affecting people employed in the trade, i.e. businessmen, shop-owners, shop assistants and trainees. It embraces relations with the local authority, shop hours, siting, redevelopment, bye-laws, relations with other traders, new and re-fitted shops, relations with the education authority, the Youth Employment Office and trade unions.

From this highly informative sheet, you will learn where to look for your interesting news items regarding any trade. Some good sources of information are trade associations, technical colleges, youth employment officers, the town hall, the Chamber of Trade courts. If you decide to attend and report on trade meetings, make sure that you give exact dates and clearly state the full identity of the organisations involved.

Personal news about the people who work within different trades is always wanted by editors who know their readers like to hear of weddings, obituaries and general gossip.

For the diary page personal anecdotes are popular so long as they are about people in the trade. Practical how-to-do-it features based on personal experience or recommendations on how to make a business appeal to customers, written from a customer's angle, would interest most editors. Keep your news items as short as possible with an average length of about 150 words.

Court cases involving the trade concerned provide useful material for trade-paper publication, i.e. damage claims by customers; prosecutions for law breaking; breaches of bye-laws, Shop Acts, etc.

The information sheet supplied by the trade press

45

editor will also give a deadline time and day for receipt of copy, and another special late time for brief reports to be followed by a fuller report in the post. They may even supply you with train times and instructions for the despatch of copy or pictures by rail when these are required the same day. If you become a regular correspondent for your district, the trade paper will often pay attendance fees to cover small, out-of-pocket expenses if these are agreed in advance.

Most information sheets contain a comprehensive list of the main trade associations covering the trade in question, together with technical colleges and trade unions. It is essential that a trade-paper writer should maintain regular contact with such organisations in his area.

Having sent for a copy of a trade paper and received one by return, read it closely, from cover to cover. This is not so easy as it sounds, as inevitably you will want to skim through the journal, reading only what catches your eye and interests you personally. You may discover that a few of the sample trade papers appeal to you more than the rest. Perhaps you have some inside information about certain trades or professions and think, after studying the style of one or two papers, that you could supply them with copy. If you take the job seriously, you will receive help from several sources. Trade-press editors are always on the look out for correspondents who can supply regular items; they will usually offer advice to any would-be contributor.

Footwear Weekly, for instance, sends out an editorial news coverage sheet, in which the editor begins:

We greatly appreciate the many news items which you have sent to us in the past, and as we are anxious to expand our news coverage, we are writing these few notes which may be helpful to you:

The following are the main types of news items which we are interested in receiving from your locality:

1. New shoe retail and repair shops opening and old ones closing down. (If possible with reasons why.)
2. News of other retailers, for instance men's outfitters, taking up the sale of shoes.
3. News of shoe people in your area: appointments; promotions; obituaries, etc., at manager, supervisor level and above.
4. Details of special retail shoe-shop promotions or advertising schemes, including special offers, cut prices, etc.
5. Details of developments in shoe factories; tanneries; shoe component suppliers in your area.
6. Anything, in fact, with a footwear interest should be submitted, including local Consumer Association reports which comment on the footwear trade.

The editor of *Footwear Weekly* then goes on to give a detailed list of rates of pay, states that he goes to press on Monday and would prefer to have all news items in the London office by the previous Friday. He adds that the earlier copy is received, the more chance there is of it being used and paid for.

The information supplied by the editor of *Footwear Weekly* could be adapted to apply to other trades and their publications. It gives a general idea of the kind of material that will interest a trade press editor, and tells an intending contributor where to look for it.

If you are ever in any doubt as to the suitability of your material for a trade paper a mutually satisfactory method of finding out is to write a brief letter giving a synopsis. In this way, you avoid unnecessary work and the editor can decide whether to give you the go ahead. It is up to you to find out what your trade-press editors require in the first instance. Cultivate a close connection with local shopkeepers and trade associations, and the copy will flow.

The American trade press
It is the ambition of most writers of novels and short stories to sell to the American markets and become a millionaire overnight. These dreams of success rarely materialise because the requirements of the American market for fiction differ widely from that in Britain.

In the trade press, however, the American editor wants much the same material as his opposite number in Britain. Readers of American trade magazines like to know what's going on within their trades and want to hear about the latest trends and developments. There are many American-owned companies with British branches and many Americans live and work in this country. If you should discover someone living and working in your area with connections with the USA, make a point of finding out all you can about his background.

When our local pet shop changed hands recently, I learned, while purchasing supplies of tinned catfood, that the new proprietor's wife was American. During a subsequent interview with the new owners, I discovered that they had met some years previously at Cruft's dog show in London, where both were showing French poodles and competing for the same awards. I wrote up the story, including references to the differences in pet-care in America and Britain. Although we British consider ourselves to be great animal lovers, it seems we fall well behind the Americans when it comes to spending money and lavishing comforts on our pets. I sent the story off to what I hoped was a suitable market in the USA. I found this listed in *Willing's Press Guide*.

Several months later I received a cheque for $30 from the American trade magazine. It will pay you to look around your home town in case you too can find an American who is engaged in some trade or business that would interest a trade magazine in the States, and to look for markets in *Willing's*.

When you have decided which trade papers to contribute to, you will slowly build up a close connection with traders and trade associations in your district, and from them you should receive plenty of copy which will interest your chosen trade journals. Be prepared to follow up anything you see, hear or read.

One day a short report in the local newspaper about two lady hairdressers caught my eye. Deciding there might be a story here suitable for *Hairdressers' Journal*, I contacted the two girls and the following copy materialised:

Two young Tyneside hairdressers, 25-year-old Joan and her assistant 29-year-old Mary started a 'dial-a-set' hairdressing business in North Shields, Northumberland, a short time ago, and their response to pleas for work to be carried out in customers' homes has been so great that they have been forced to open a salon.

'We were so busy that we had to open a salon at — which used to be called "Marilyn",' said Mary. Some weeks, the couple work four nights until 11 pm each night, travelling anything up to ten miles from their salon, complete with mobile hairdressing equipment. 'Not only do we have one customer in a household,' said Mary, 'but we find that often friends and neighbours arrive to join the hairdressing "party". We also visit customers who cannot leave their homes because of accidents and crippling diseases. We both feel we are giving a good service to our customers and they have repaid us by giving us more orders than we can comfortably fill.'

Watch out for newly opened shops for these are always of interest to the trade paper concerned. Going home from work one night I spotted a newly opened teenage fashionwear boutique. I called in for a chat with the owners, and besides providing the copy for the *Drapery and Fashion Weekly* and *Draper's Record,* the story also made a gossip item for the local evening newspaper.

Even when disaster strikes, it can provide pounds and pence for the trade press writer. *Carpet News Weekly* published the following story under the heading 'Broken Main Swamps Carpet Showroom'.

When the staff of — Ltd. arrived at work last Monday at their — store, they got a shock. The basement, which has one of the largest carpet showrooms in Britain, with over £50,000 worth of stock, was under at least one foot of water. The firm has estimated that there was more than £10,000 worth of damage to carpets, Chinese rugs and other items. The water had seeped into the building when a water main broke on a nearby building site. Lighting was switched off because of the fire hazard, but business carried on as usual in the rest of the store.

From reading the foregoing examples of trade-press journalism, you will realise that once you become aware of the potential worth of small everyday items of news that come to your ears, you will not find it difficult to earn regular cheques from being a trade-press contributor. This is a branch of writing which is very often overlooked by the freelance and yet the possibilities of success are very great. Trade editors are extremely co-operative and helpful. Just to whet your appetite, here are some of the trade-press markets to which I contribute. There are hundreds more waiting for you to discover them for yourself.

Some trade-press markets

Pram Retailer
Timber Trade's Journal
British Baker
Bakers' Review
Motor Trader
Carpet Review
Grocers' Gazette
The Grocer
Tailor and Cutter
Meat Trade's Journal
Fruit, Flower and Vegetable Trade's Journal
The Florist
Fish Trade's Gazette
Footwear Weekly
Men's Wear
Draper and Fashion Weekly
Off-Licence Journal
Pet Trade Journal
Waste Trade Review

Drapers' Record
Chemist and Druggist
Retail Chemist
Retail Newsagent
National Newsagent
Confectionery and Tobacco News
The Triple Trader
Nursing Mirror
Nursing Times
Catering Times
Caterer and Hotelkeeper
Hardware Trade Journal
Hairdressers' Journal
Jeweller
Knitting and Haberdashery Review
Optician
Watchmaker, Jeweller and Silversmith

6—Writing for the Women's Page

Beryl Sandwell

Most local newspapers and several of the dailies include a regular page or section for their women readers, and although many of the articles published may be written by staff writers, a considerable amount of material is supplied by the freelance contributor. A glance at the women's page in your local newspaper will show you the kind of short article that is required, and if you are interested in the district where you live, and your neighbours and local activities, you may like to try your hand at becoming a women's page contributor. Most newspapers employ a full time women's editor, who relies on freelance contributors to fill up her pages each week.

Subjects for the women's page

There may be a great deal of space given up to reports of weddings, social gatherings and meetings; there may also be regular features that appear each week. One of these might be a 'Recipe of the Week' or a 'Topical Home Hint'; there is probably a gardening piece and perhaps one written on that week's TV programmes. Most of these short articles will be sent in by freelance contributors, and if you carefully study your own local women's page you will soon discover the kind of piece they print. You will also see what is lacking and perhaps have ideas that may interest the women's page

53

editor. A friend of mine who kept forgetting the dates of local events suggested that a list of forthcoming events published regularly in the local paper would be a great memory-jogger to people like herself. For some time now she has been supplying her paper with a regular feature called 'Where shall we go this week?' It lists coffee mornings, wine-and-cheese parties, swimming galas, jumble sales, fashion shows, local sales, lectures, school sports' days, garden fetes, etc., in fact any event to be held locally that might interest women readers.

Another friend of mine, keen on local history, approached her local newspaper asking if they would be interested in publishing a series of short articles on local places of historical interest. She received an enthusiastic letter of acceptance and a contract by return of post.

These articles are usually quite short, 250 to 800 words. They must of course be primarily of interest to women, though not necessarily purely domestic. After studying your local women's page, jot down your ideas and write or call to see your local women's page editor. You will probably find that she will be delighted to receive your suggestions, especially if you are able to provide something that the column lacks.

As it would be physically impossible for the women's page editor to go to every social function in the district in order to report on it, you may find that she will pay you to write up reports of events that you have to attend. Do you attend a flower arranging class or a women's club where you have notable speakers? If so, take your notebook along with you next time you go, and submit a report to your paper. In order to avoid duplicating reports, it is advisable to contact your women's page editor before attending the event, asking if someone is already lined up to cover it. Be businesslike in your dealings with the editor, and find out the rate to be paid for your articles before you send them in. Find out too when the editor wants your work to be on her desk, ready for publication day. Remember, when your enthusiasm for your subject runs away with you, that space available for your piece in the paper will be at a premium, and your work will stand a better chance of being included if you keep your articles short, informative and to the point. There is no room for flowery phrases and long-winded descriptions.

If your editor shows a cautious interest in your ideas, then waste no time in submitting a sample of your work. Remember that topicality always counts in a newspaper article, and that items of local interest will be more acceptable than the general interest piece.

Interviews with interesting women personalities living in your district are particularly appealing to the women's page editor. Suggest several of these, and find out if the editor wants a picture to go alongside the feature. The women's page editor will then arrange for a staff photographer to go along to the home of your featured personality to obtain the necessary pictures.

For a women's page, articles about children and their activities, health, hobbies and idiosyncracies are always welcome. Try sending articles about interesting local children to your women's page. In my home town, we have a girl swimmer who has reached international standard, a boy actor who is obviously going places and another boy who takes part in Continental bicycle road races. All of them have been written about extensively on the women's page of our local newspaper. If you think your editor would be interested in hearing more about youngsters making a name for themselves in your area, watch out for snippets of news about them in local news items, and then suggest to your editor that women readers would like to hear more about these children. You may start by submitting one article and end up doing a series, spurred on by the thought of receiving a regular cheque for your efforts. If you do make a niche for yourself with a permanent place on your women's page, make a point of being reliable so that the editor knows that your copy will be on her desk promptly each week.

Keep your diary handy and look up forthcoming holidays and important dates. Most small towns and villages have special yearly events originally started by local residents in the past; a few hundred words written about the history of such events will make an interesting item. Read up your local history, get the names right, check the dates and wait for your piece to appear in the next issue of your local rag.

Are you good at crosswords? Why not try your hand at compiling one for your women's page? Give the clues a local slant wherever possible to add to the interest. If this proves to be popular with women readers, you might persuade your editor to offer a small prize for the first correct entry opened each week.

Are you a budding poet? If so, you will know that poetry is not easy to sell these days. But poems about local events and places might interest an editor. Why not try to make a market for your poetry in your local paper? You may be as lucky as a friend of mine who regularly expresses, in verse, her comments on local activities. These are often topical in content; every time local opinion and voices are raised in protest, my friend puts it down in humorous verse. Her poems comment on the weather, the bad condition of the roads, local politics and the new supermarket in the main street. Each time something newsworthy happens in the town, we all quickly turn to the women's page each Friday to see what our poet makes of things! Try your hand if poetry is your thing.

Has your local paper got a column about books? Or a 'Children's Corner'? If not, why not? Writing for your local women's page is something anybody can achieve, and you never know where that first, short article will lead you. It is easier to write about people and places familiar to you than to tackle articles requiring a lot of careful research. With your local newspaper, you are on your home ground. Use your friends. Ask them what they would like to read in their women's page. Try out your ideas on them before submitting them to the editor. Get them to ring you up giving details of forthcoming events of which they have prior knowledge. You will find, after a very short time, that people begin to know that you write for the local newspaper, and they will be eager to help you gather information. Never be afraid to ring up professional people for help; in most instances this will be readily forthcoming.

Once it becomes known that you are interested in local events, you will find yourself receiving countless invitations from different organisations to attend functions as a representative of the local press. You will be wined and dined and be expected to pay for your dinner by producing a write-up, with pictures, in next week's edition of the local paper. If this happens to you, do remember that your women readers will be particularly interested in the dresses worn by the ladies, especially the guests and dignitaries at the top table. Describe in great detail what the lady speaker wore and much of what she said, and include information about the menu served. Don't worry about producing your notebook during the proceedings, for this is necessary if you are to get your facts right.

You may find, with experience, that many professional speakers will be prepared to hand you a copy of their notes, if you ask for it. This means that you do not have to work so hard, and also ensures that you get your facts right when you are making your report the next day.

When your first pieces are published on your local women's page, study them carefully to see if they have been altered in any way. Almost invariably you will find your efforts are ruthlessly pruned by the editor. Don't take this to heart. Remember that the editor knows what space can be spared for your article, and in almost every item written there are superfluous words and sentences that can be cut out, if necessary, without altering the context. It is better to have your work pruned and printed than to have it discarded altogether.

Besides the many local newspapers printed each week, several of the large dailies accept work from freelance contributors. These newspapers, on the whole, are interested in the authoritative article written by someone who is a specialist in a certain subject; alternatively they will take the personal experience article. If you have climbed a mountain hitherto unconquered, escaped from prison through some special ingenuity or discovered a new substitute for rubber, then the women's page editors of *The Times,* the *Telegraph* or the *Guardian* would be interested in your achievement. Articles written for the dailies run to 1000 or 1500 words, and they pay well for suitable material.

Type your article using double-spacing on A4 paper, remembering to put your name and address at the top right-hand corner. Choose a short, pithy title to catch the editor's eye, and underline it. She may not use it, but it may serve to make her give your work a second look. Your title should relate to the article's contents, using as few words as possible. A good idea when trying to decide on a title is to spend a little time studying the published titles used in the magazine or newspaper where you hope to place your work. The style and type of article headings used by different editors will help you in your choice of that all-important title.

Varying rates are paid by newspapers up and down the country. In the first instance, as a beginner, accept whatever you are offered, and then when you have proved yourself capable of producing the kind of material your women's page editor likes to feature in her pages, ask for an increase in pay. Newspapers calculate payments to freelance contributors based on the number of lines taken up by an item in a column.

Two examples of published women's page articles

A HANDFUL OF HERBS

Have you ever wondered why your pot roasts, soups or sauces never taste the same as those served by your favourite restaurant? Or paused to ponder, as you swallowed your antibiotics, how our forefathers dealt with minor ailments when doctors were scarce and penicillin unheard of?

The answer lies in the use of herbs; used knowledgeably they can add variety and piquancy to the most ordinary dish. The cultivated types are generally used for cooking, whilst the wild herbs of the countryside were used—and still are in some remote country districts—for their healing and antiseptic properties.

Anybody with a tiny piece of spare ground can grow a herb garden. Parsley, fennel, marjoram and chervil are best treated as annuals and grown each year from seeds sown in the spring. Bay is an evergreen tree, while mint, rosemary, chives and sage are perennial and once established from a cutting or root division will soon form strong clumps.

The leaves of all herbs can be picked from spring to autumn, and used freshly plucked. They can also be picked, dried and stored for winter use.

Herbs should be gathered on a dry day, using only fresh, unmarked leaves—a warm summer's day is the best time to choose. Dry either in a slow oven or in warm sunshine until crisp, then rub between your hands into airtight storage jars. Wild herbs are dried in the same way, though they must be carefully washed beforehand. In some herbs, the roots and flowers are used, as well as the leaves, and these are dried in the same way.

Facts and uses of culinary and medicinal herbs

Rosemary:	Grown from seed or cuttings. Perennial, with fragrant, spiky leaves and pale blue flowers. Add to chicken and pea soups; to cheese and white sauces and scrambled eggs.
Chives:	Perennial, resembling tiny onion. Start from one bulb and clump will soon develop. An excellent garnish for creamed vegetables, fish and omelettes. Chop finely and mix with cream cheese for sandwich filler.
Bay:	An evergreen tree—leaves only are used. Grow from young plant—slips may be successful in the south. Fine seasoning to add to stews, pot roasts and tomato soup. Add to water when cooking carrots or tomatoes.

Tarragon:	Perennial, but may require protection in winter in northern districts. Start from root division. Sprinkle over omelettes, scrambled eggs or baked fish dishes. Put in water when cooking broccoli or cabbage.
Sage:	Perennial, hardy, enjoying full sun. Grow from seed or cuttings. Add a pinch to sausages, stews, gravies and cheese spread. Stuff rabbit as well as poultry, and add to cooking water of brussels sprouts, onions and peas.

Some of the wild herbs used in the treatment of ailments are easily recognisable in the hedgerows, and a chat with a countryman will often help in the observation and search for them. Whether leaves, flowers or roots are used, the general method was to simmer a handful of the dried herbs in water, and drink the resulting liquid; one handful to a quart.

Camomile:	Medicinal. Perennial white flower with yellow centre and trailing, branched stems. Very abundant in Cornwall and other parts of England. Used for neuralgia and may also be added to poultices and fomentations.
Bryony:	A climbing plant found in hedges. Its red berries are very poisonous. A potion made from the roots was used for coughs and colds.
Plantain:	A common weed known to most gardeners, with thick oval leaves and inconspicuous green, spiked flowers. Leaves were rubbed on stings. Root

61

	and seed used to treat diarrhoea and dysentery.
Dandelion:	The common, yellow-flowered plant. Leaves used widely for blood conditions and disorders of liver and kidney.
Elder:	A small tree bearing clusters of white flowers and dark purple berries. The flowers were used for sore throat and inflammation.
Marshmallow:	Grows on marshes and near the sea, has flesh-coloured flowers and downy leaves and stem. The white, fleshy, carrot-shaped root used for coughs.

UNACCUSTOMED AS I AM . . . .

You may avoid it for a year or two, but sooner or later, however shy and retiring you are, someone is going to get you up on a platform with a sea of faces at your feet, and you are going to have to take a deep breath, swat the butterflies in your tummy, and speak in public for the first time in your life. It may be at a Young Farmer's Club or a W I evening, but however small or unimportant your individual contribution, a few basic do's and don't are essential, if the event is going to be painless for both you and your audience!

Having agreed on your subject with the person in charge, find out how long you will be expected to speak, the general type and age of your audience, and any particular points you will be expected to touch on, or to avoid, in your speech. I am assuming that you know your subject and have swotted up on any facts about which you feel hazy.

First write out the complete speech and speak it aloud in order to time yourself. Do not, however, read your speech from the platform; this can be very dreary, however interesting your subject; the best of audiences will soon become tired of looking at the top of your bowed head. Make some notes of the important facts in your speech, and don't be afraid to stop and glance at them if you are momentarily at a loss. Once you are back on the track, talk slowly, easily, in your everyday voice. The most successful speakers are the ones who behave naturally, without affectation.

If you make a mistake or drop your notes, don't panic; correct yourself or pick up your notes with a smile. Remember that sort of thing can happen to all of us, and an audience warms to a speaker with the human touch.

Although you talk naturally and clearly to your audience, do not look at them. Address yourself to the back wall, smile at it if you like—avoid catching anyone's eye if you do not want the rest of your speech to go hurtling out of your head.

A further word about those notes in your hand—write a few relevant words clearly, preferably on a stiff postcard. You will not have the time to read through the whole sentence, but a single word can often bring the truant thoughts racing back into a blank mind.

Try to look confident even though you feel like crawling under the nearest stone; if your ego needs a boost, wear something new—a mint-fresh suit or a stunning new hat will interest your audience, even if your speech does not! It also works wonders for your wilting confidence.

If you have to use a microphone, stand at the correct distance, with your face about six inches away, and speak in your normal voice. Keep a pleasant, interested expression pinned to your face both while delivering your speech, and during the preliminary formalities. Ascertain the names of your chairman and other personalities before the fateful day, so that you can refer to them naturally, if necessary.

Talk clearly and slowly, varying your pace occasionally; we all know how dreary a droning voice can become. Keep one eye on the time, and when you have said your piece, finish smartly and sit down. Do not hum and haw and keep mumbling on. The beginning and ending of your speech must both be crisp—spend a lot of time and thought on making them just right.

One last word about your hands and feet—the things which so often bother a speaker. Find a pose which is comfortable, and if you move occasionally to gesture or demonstrate a point, go back to your comfortable pose afterwards. Knowing that you have found a comfortable and suitable position will help you to feel better.

Above all, do not fiddle with your handbag, gloves or the bobbles on the tablecloth! Don't gnaw your nails or play with your hair because you are nervous. Don't worry about the impression your speech has made on the audience, because you will never please everybody. Just remember your new suit or that sensational creation you are wearing on your head, and relax. After all, if your audience did not care for your carefully prepared speech, they have certainly had their money's-worth out of your pretty, chic appearance!

7—Writing for the Radio

Beryl Sandwell

Although at times it seems that television has taken over from radio, writers should remember that there is still a vast audience that listens regularly. Housewives busy with their chores during the day, retired people, invalids and pre-school children are all able to switch on regularly to enjoy radio programmes. The BBC national network, the local BBC stations broadcasting on VHF and commercial radio all offer opportunities to the freelance writer. At the present time, of these three, local radio offers the best chance to the beginner; new stations are constantly starting up, and although payment may not be great, the experience of writing for broadcasting is invaluable.

The short radio talk is the easiest and shortest way to success in radio writing and any normally literate person should be able to produce any number of suitable pieces.

Tips on writing a radio talk or story

Sincerity is the keynote of radio writing. Consider your audience, remembering that your listener may be doing a job of work while listening. Capture his interest in your first arresting sentence, remembering that it is very easy for a bored listener to switch off. Find out which local radio station serves your home locality and listen regularly to the programmes. Several local stations are interested in broadcasting short stories by local writers as well as talks. These generally occupy from five to fifteen minutes on the air. Radio Bristol, for instance, broadcasts two each week at the present time, length 850 words, for an initial fee of £3. If your local station has a similar spot for fiction, why not try your hand at story writing? Giving your tale a local background, using familiar street names and giving your characters surnames that are common in your area will add to its appeal. Set your tale against landmarks your audience will easily recognise—a well-known park or factory landscape—familiar events, discos and department stores.

Are you an expert on some subject? Write it up in an interesting, informative manner and cash in on your expertise. Such talks should be between five and twelve minutes in length, and may be on a wide range of subjects slanted to suit varying audiences at different times of day.

Talks specially written for your local radio station are invariably on topics of interest to people living in the area. In order to discover just what goes out on the air, listen regularly. Study the opportunities available before sending in your script. Use a watch to time the length of talks that are most popular with your local producer. Remember that it is the policy of many of these local stations to broadcast only scripts received by people living in their particular area, and your chances of success in this field are much greater than in the national BBC network programmes. Radio Blackburn, for instance, regularly broadcasts stories for children and adults, and poems contributed by local writers.

Listeners are always interested to hear about other people's jobs. Yours might not seem very interesting to you, but it may fascinate a listener. Margaret Powell's stories of life below stairs are now famous, and I remember once hearing a broadcast talk given by an ambulance driver who delivered his first baby on the platform of a London underground station during an air raid. Another example was a talk given by a young policeman relating his feelings and experiences after his first night on the beat.

Be on the look-out for the unusual character. I once sat next to a bowler-hatted, brief-cased businessman in a crowded station buffet while we waited for an overdue train. He had me riveted to my seat when he told me confidentially that he had once belonged to a Liverpool gang that had planned and successfully carried off several bankraids. I don't know whether he was telling the truth or not, but his story earned me several pounds when written up into a five minute radio talk.

Try to keep the mood of your writing light whenever possible, and avoid references to disease and death.

The title of your radio talk is vitally important as it often provides the key to the content without giving anything away. Imagine it appearing in the *Radio Times,* and make sure it will entice a listener to switch on. Don't try to be too clever, however, for the obscure reference is lost when the words are read or heard just once and never again. There can be no turning back the page for your radio listener, and therefore it should be the writer's aim to communicate simply, with crisp, clear sentences.

Most short talks written specially for broadcasting are read aloud by their writers, so be prepared to do this when sending in your script. Long words and involved sentences may look fine on paper, but may prove to be tongue-twisters and boring to a listener. Rambling sentences full of flowery descriptions may be enjoyable to write, but they will not impress your listener; they will merely send him to sleep or to switch off.

As you are writing your talk, forget about grammar, spelling or searching for an unusual word. When working on your first draft, imagine that you are writing to a friend, telling him your story. Use the same simple words and phraseology you would use in normal speech. Let the words flow from your pen as they come into your mind and get them down. There will be plenty of time later to tidy up mistakes in spelling or grammar, and if you write as you speak, your work will sound refreshingly entertaining. There will be pace and enthusiasm in your talk that would be lost if you deliberated over every word. Don't merely tell your listeners what happened to you—explain how it made you *feel,* so that they will sympathise with you in your difficulties, and rejoice over your successes.

When you are trying to think up an interesting subject for your radio talk, it may be of help if you realise that the things you don't know or can't do are as fascinating to your listeners as those you do know and can do. You win a sympathetic ear just because you don't know it all. Your listeners are cheered to discover they are not the only ones who are hopeless at mastering the simplest task.

'But what do *you* know about diving?' jeered my family when a contract and cheque arrived for a talk I'd written on the subject. 'I know how *not* to do it!' I retorted, still smarting from innumerable abortive attempts to land head first in the pool instead of flat on my stomach.

Keeping your radio talk as short as possible increases its chances of acceptance. A producer may squeeze in a five-minute piece when he will not look twice at one that runs to fifteen minutes, however interesting or well-written it is. Count the words carefully when your talk is done, allowing approximately 150 words per reading minute.

In writing for your local radio remember always that the emphasis is on *local* affairs and personalities. Short news items or reports on parochial events will usually interest the producer. There may be a regular religious spot to which you could contribute. Local history students have at their fingertips a wealth of information to impart to local audiences. If you have an idea for a certain type of programme, write a short note to the producer giving a brief outline and asking for his comments. If your idea appeals to him, you may discover that you have carved a special niche for yourself on your local radio programme.

Because radio is such a personal medium, talks and stories come over best when written in the first person. Even strictly factual articles sound more interesting when they include references to the writer's own experiences.

If you do succeed in writing and selling a short story to your local radio station, don't be surprised if the producer asks a professional actor to read it over the air. Even though you may think you would prefer to read your own work, the truth is that a professional will make a better job of doing justice to your tale. This is also true of the stories written for the BBC regular fifteen-minute Morning Story, broadcast on Radio 4, Monday to Friday at 10.45. I know from personal experience that the actor chosen is invariably able to bring warmth to the characters and a pace to the plot that would be lost had I been allowed to read my own story.

Reading your script
In the case of a talk, however, for both the BBC national network or local radio, you will almost cer-

tainly be expected to read your script. If you own a tape recorder, use it at home to hear how your talk will sound over the air; it is useful also for timing the length of your talk, and to help you develop an easy, relaxed style when talking aloud. At first you may be inclined to gabble the words at a rapid pace; alternatively you may sound stilted and nervous. A little practice will boost your confidence and get you used to the sound of your own voice.

Being asked to a studio to record something you have written is one of the perks of the job, and even if you develop a butterfly-tummy when confronted by a microphone for the first time, you will thoroughly enjoy the experience.

Because a radio studio has to be sound-proof, the walls are often padded, the floor close-carpeted to cut down noise, and there are usually no windows. There may also be floor-length curtains to deaden unwanted sounds. All this can give you a feeling of claustrophobia and a sensation of being cut off from the outside world which may add to your nervousness. However, you will soon get used to this and also the strangely flat sound that your own voice makes in the quietness. Naturally, you will try to vary your tone and pitch and pace during the recording, to avoid sounding monotonous and dreary. Don't be afraid to pause and take a breath. Read your script as though you were chatting to a friend. Don't try to learn it off by heart, for this is quite unnecessary. You will be sitting at a table covered in green baize with the unpinned pages of your script in front of you, alongside the microphone, and each time you reach the bottom of a page, drop it to the floor beside you. In this way, you will avoid rustling the pages, a sound that the microphone can pick up and intensify.

70

If you should stumble over a word, don't panic. Pause for a couple of seconds, and then begin the sentence again. Later, your mistake will be edited out of the recording, and the correct sentence left in its place.

BBC programmes on the national network such as Woman's Hour and You and Yours occasionally accept scripts from the freelance, although broadcasters need to be highly specialised in their subjects. Much of the programme content is instant and up-to-date, and there is little scope for the beginner. The commercial radio stations now being launched may provide additional outlets for your work. Tune in regularly and give some study to the programmes being broadcast, so that you have a fair idea of the type of material used before you submit a script.

For BBC national network programmes, fees are assessed on the basis of the type of material, its length and the author's status and experience in writing for radio. Minimum fees range from £1.45 a minute for talks. Local radio fees appear to vary in different regions depending on the budgets available, but there are signs that these fees are gradually increasing. The same applies to commercial radio, and the freelance should enquire what fee is being offered before allowing work to be broadcast. Never, in any circumstances, agree to receive no payment for your radio script however tempted you may be by the prospect of hearing your work over the air. To do so would merely debase the standard of fees for every other writer.

For a page of specimen script along with information about the requirements of the BBC, send for the valuable publication *Writing for the BBC*. This is a guide for writers on possible markets for their work within the BBC, and is obtainable through booksellers or from BBC Publications, 35, Marylebone High St., London

W1M 4AA. Local radio stations in your own area are listed in the *Radio Times* and full programmes of your own particular local radio are included in every edition.

A full list of all addresses of BBC national regions and local radio stations is to be found in the *Writers' and Artists' Year Book* under the chapter on broadcasting. Details of commercial sound radio stations may be obtained from the Independent Broadcasting Authority, address in the *Writers' and Artists' Year Book.*

An example of a script written for radio. (Originally broadcast in the BBC programme Motoring and the Motorist.)

THE RIGHT APPROACH
(Reading time approximately six minutes)

I really can't understand why men make such a fuss when their wives tell them they're taking up driving. After all, when you've produced and reared a couple of children, moved house half a dozen times and learned how to mend a fuse, driving a car seems like child's play.

Men are so emotional about the whole thing; mention traffic wardens, policemen or second hand car dealers and they threaten to burst a blood vessel. Any woman will tell you that their whole approach is wrong.

There is no doubt that cars and driving hold a strange fascination for men. It starts when they are in rompers, zooming round their nurseries in a pedal car and doesn't seem to desert them this side of the grave. Once bitten by the motoring bug, men seem to become intoxicated by the feeling of power they experience when driving a car. Think of all the meek, harmless little men who become roaring maniacs when behind the steering wheel. Perfectly sane, conventional males blossom out into loud checked caps and yellow string gloves; they drive much too fast and become raving lunatics when overtaken by small decrepit sports cars.

Women, being by nature more rational and matter-of-fact, regard cars as useful pieces of home equipment designed to make life easier and more pleasant. They don't think it essential to know what goes on under the bonnet any more than to understand how a fridge works. When women climb into the driving seat, all they require is to be taken uneventfully and at a moderate speed to their destinations. They object to punctures, blocked carburettors, noisy exhaust pipes, winkers that won't wink and men who think women drivers are the end.

And once a woman has decided to learn to drive, it takes more than the feeble excuses trotted out by a mere male to deter her.

, When I told my husband that I thought I'd learn to drive, he shot out of his chair and wanted to know why I'd waited until he had exchanged our old 1948 saloon before dropping that bombshell. He went on to produce a dozen ridiculous reasons why I should remain in the passenger seat for the rest of my life, but he could have saved his breath.

I hung my 'L' plates fore and aft of our brand new saloon and stood back to admire the effect. Then, armed with my crisp new provisional licence, and my head spinning with driving tips, I climbed nonchalantly into the driving seat and prepared to drive the car out of the garage.

I can't adequately explain the extraordinary behaviour of the car during the next few moments. Maybe it had overheard my husband muttering unrepeatable things about women drivers—he does this frequently. At any rate, the car jerked, roared, bucked

73

and backfired without moving an inch forward. I decided to ignore this sulkiness, and this was obviously the right approach, because, quick as a flash, the car leapt for the gatepost and demolished it.

Isn't it odd how quickly a crowd of grinning males will appear from nowhere when a woman prangs a car? In two seconds they had tipped me out of the driving seat, shoved the car neatly back into the garage, and carried my white-lipped husband off to the local for a reviving pint.

The insurance man and the local garage hands were perfectly sweet and helpful about paying for the damage and fixing the crumpled radiator. There was absolutely no reason at all for my husband's coldness towards me during the following week. When my next driving lesson came round, there was only the pile of bricks at the drive entrance to remind anyone of my first unfortunate lesson. My husband had categorically refused to build it up again until I passed my test.

As though the car regretted our first encounter, my second lesson began very smoothly. The car seemed to have become resigned to the feel of my hands on the wheel, and it behaved quietly and docilely as we proceeded out of the drive and down the avenue towards the main road. I wish I could say the same for my husband; he crouched beside me giving a fair imitation of a half-set jelly. His frenzied instructions to brake, accelerate, signal, change down or stop, ricochetted around inside my head. Only a woman could remain calm under such provocation. I even found myself experiencing a delicious, heady feeling when I shifted into top gear and felt the car leap forward. Our family saloon was behaving impeccably; it even had the good sense to stop abruptly when the traffic lights turned red right under its front wheels. It did stall, however, in mild protest, and while the lights changed from red to amber, to green, and back to red, I was busily pulling the starter, checking that the handbrake was on and the gear lever in neutral. When the cars behind began making rude noises on their horns, my husband swore in a very ungentlemanly manner and jumped out!

Afterwards he insisted firmly to me, and also to the policeman who witnessed his act of desertion, that he only meant to exchange seats with me. Unfortunately, as soon as he slammed the nearside door, the engine jumped into life, and the car and I roared across the road against the lights, narrowly missing a large laundry van before mounting a traffic island and coming to rest before the aforesaid policeman.

It was most fortunate that we came across such a sensible, pleasant policeman. He was very understanding when I explained about being a learner, and feeling terribly nervous when my husband was criticising every single move I made. He agreed that no damage had been done apart from a microscopic scratch on the car door where it had brushed with the traffic island, and when I'd apologised abjectly about a dozen times, he let me off with a caution; he even offered to give me a few lessons when he was off duty after he had witnessed my husband's hysteria at the sight of the microscopic scratch on the door.

As I told my husband when I'd passed the driving test at my first attempt, all you needed was the right approach. Car driving requires a cool head in emergencies, patience and forbearance when dealing with the public or the police, and a modicum of sound commonsense such as all women naturally possess—and very few men, at least where a car is concerned.

I felt quite sad at having to remove my rather battered 'L' plates, but as I said at the beginning, I really can't understand why men make such a fuss when their wives decide to take up driving. Can you?

8—Women's Magazine Stories

Beryl Sandwell

One of the best ways to earn cash from writing is to enter the women's magazine fiction field. A glance at the bookstall on your local railway station will give you some idea of the number of publications, both weekly and monthly, for women of differing age groups and interests. Teenagers, young marrieds, career girls and older women are all catered for, and most of these magazines publish short stories. These tales all have wide appeal and follow certain rules which you, as a beginner, must learn and follow, if you aim to sell your work:

1. The characters in your stories must be ordinary people, not millionaires or foreign princesses.
2. What happens to your characters might, the reader must feel, happen to herself or at least to people she knows.
3. How your characters react to these happenings must be in a way your reader thinks she would react to similar circumstances, and so your story becomes believable.

Modern women's magazine stories are deceptively simple. Have you ever picked up a copy of *My Weekly* or *Woman's Own*, read one of the stories, and thought that you could produce something equally good, if not better? If this is how the stories strike you, you may be sure that the writers have worked hard to achieve this apparent simplicity. The plots of these stories are often quite slight and it is the clever characterisation that makes them appealing to the reader.

Now, having decided to try your hand at this very lucrative type of writing, what is the first step? Remember that it is useless to write stories that appeal only to yourself. The editors of women's magazines are competent businessmen. They know who their readers are and exactly what they want to read. Your first job is to buy a selection of the women's magazines, read every word in them, including the advertisements, and decide which one to aim for. Many beginners fail to realise that every single woman's magazine has requirements that differ slightly from those of its competitors. A short story published in *Woman* would never sell to *She* and a story written for *Woman's Weekly* would not be suitable for readers of *19*.

Before setting out to write for any one of the women's magazines, you must read the type of fiction published by its editor. Don't be like a would-be writer I once met who, after telling me she was trying to write women's magazine fiction, added: 'Of course, I never read them myself. They're not my sort of thing at all!'

If you want to be able to write and sell to a particular magazine, it is only sensible to find out the kind of story it requires. Buy the magazine regularly, read the stories carefully and critically, until you feel you know why the editor bought them. The best way to find out his requirements is to read the stories *he has already paid for.* Now this simple truth is sometimes difficult for new writers to swallow. They trot out various excuses when their stories fail to sell: the editor doesn't recognise good work when he sees it; he only buys from writers who are well-known; he has his favourites whose work appears frequently in the magazine. None of these things is true. The fact is that editors of women's magazines are always in need of good stories, and if you can write what they want, they will welcome you with wide-open arms, and pay you handsomely.

When you're eager to make a start, when a splendid plot is seething in your mind, it isn't easy to accept the fact that your story hasn't a hope of achieving publication unless it fulfils exactly the editor's requirements. If he wants family stories of not more than 3,000 words with happy endings, then he won't consider publishing your 6,000 word science fiction mystery, however brilliantly it is written.

Producing what the editor wants

Remember that the editor has a job to do—that is, he has to know what his readers like, and to provide this, so that they will continue to buy his magazine. If he doesn't please his readers, he will soon be out of a job. So do remember if an editor rejects your first attempts at fiction, it is simply because you have not yet succeeded in producing what he wants.

So, how does the beginner find out what any editor will buy? Studying the market he hopes to write for is something every successful short-story writer does regularly as part of the job. You must train yourself to pick out important points that are common to all stories in a particular magazine. Here are ten questions to help you discover an editor's needs. After reading a story in the magazine you hope to write for, make a note of the following:

1. What is the average length of the stories?
2. How many characters are there? Male and female?
3. What are the ages of the main characters?

79

4. What are the professions of the people in the story? Plumbers or poets?
5. Are the characters mainly single—at school or college—working girls or married with children? Or are they elderly with grown-up children? Divorced or widowed?
6. Is the story ending happy or merely hopeful? Or is it a surprise and entirely unexpected?
7. Is a foreign background often used? Do the characters live in London or Scotland or the provinces? Town or country?
8. What are the names of the characters? Are they normal, everyday ones like John and Jane, or unusual like Andreana and Reuben?
9. Are the stories written in the first person, viz.: 'I sipped my martini and watched Paul walk out of the room and out of my life.' Or in the third person, viz.: 'Jenny stood with the drink in her hand while Paul strode away from her.' Or does the magazine use stories written in both first and third person narrative?
10. How many stories are published each week/month.

After applying the above questionnaire to several short stories, you will find that a pattern will emerge. One editor may use lots of stories around 4,000 words long, written in the first person, with characters in their early twenties, usually unmarried and career-minded, and there is always a happy ending. When you have discovered these important facts, you are all set to begin your own story, incorporating these points.

Here I would like to mention something of vital interest to a new writer. After doing your market study you will have discovered that some magazines publish just one short story per month whilst others use five or six each week. It is only sensible, therefore, to aim for a market where your chances of success are greater. Remember that until you sell that first story, you won't feel like a real writer, so make it easier for yourself by writing the type of story that has a better chance of selling. You may think you'd like to write for *Homes and Gardens,* but they only publish twelve stories a year, so when you are a beginner, try first to write for one of the weekly magazines that includes four or five stories every week.

Each short story that appears in print contains certain ingredients which are absolutely essential, and when starting to write for the women's magazines, you must make sure your stories include all these vital elements.

Ingredients of a saleable short story
1. An interesting, absorbing plot
2. Characters who are likeable and true-to-life
3. Natural-sounding dialogue
4. Emotion
5. Suspense
6. Reader identification
7. A satisfactory ending

We must work through these ingredients one by one. First, the interesting, absorbing plot. New writers sometimes find great difficulty in thinking up new plots. It seems they've all been done before. What is there new to say? They rack their brains, dreaming up fantastic and complicated plots, but this, on the whole, is quite unnecessary. Of course, your plot must be sound, well thought out, and realistic, but if you have done your market study you will have found out that most modern women's magazine stories rely for their originality on some new twist or inversion of circumstances. The old 'boy meets girl' themes still sell, but the problems at the heart of the stories must be contemporary. Your tale will stand a better chance of achieving publication if you choose a modern theme, one that may be common to many of your readers; a girl who has lost her job through being unpunctual and unreliable; a woman who wakes up one morning convinced that there is no real purpose in her life; a young wife of a highly successful young executive who is suddenly made redundant.

Now, you are probably saying to yourself, these themes are so ordinary, they've been done time and time again. And of course you are right. The problems at the heart of women's magazine stories do not change very much. It is your individual way of coping with it, your neat and convincing solution that makes your story seem mint-fresh to your reader.

Don't confuse ideas with complete plots. Take one of the themes given above—the girl who has lost her job through being unpunctual—that is the idea, the first spark that sets your mind working. You must turn that spark into a complete story. It is your job to decide how the girl will deal with her problem. Will she change her ways, having learnt her lesson, or will she find herself a job where the hours are more suited to her temperament? How does it affect her when she loses the job? Does she care? Does she tell her parents? Or her hard-working boy-friend? Perhaps they quarrel because they are both supposed to be saving hard to get married and the boy-friend considers the girl has acted irresponsibly. How do you think the story will work out? Having decided on the basic problem round which your story is to be written, before you start writing, do have some idea how you are going to end the story. Don't begin until you are quite sure how your plot will unfold. Make notes on possible incidents you'd like to use. Jot down those marvellous phrases that keep flitting through your head and that snappy bit of dialogue you overheard in the supermarket queue and mean to use in your story. You can concentrate on those later when your story is clear in your mind. Think about your characters when you're washing up or driving the children to school. You'll be surprised how ideas and solutions plop into your head at the oddest moments.

Where to find plots
One point I must make quite clear is that successful, prolific writers of short stories do not sit around waiting for inspiration. Plots do not work themselves out in your head without any effort on your part. The basic idea, however, may present itself to you at any time. You simply have to learn to recognise a good idea for a story when you see it.

Keep a notebook always at the ready and jot down anything that you think might make a story. People like to talk about themselves and their problems, so train yourself to listen and remember. Perhaps your neighbour pops in for a coffee and as you chat she tells you she is worried because her child refuses to eat green vegetables and her husband insists that the child must eat up before leaving the table. Every meal becomes a battlefield, she tells you. You can imagine the conflict between husband and wife and decide for yourself how the problem will be solved. Probably your ending will be entirely different from the one your neighbours decide upon. She gives you the idea, and you turn it into a plot with a satisfying ending.

Look in your daily newspaper for plot ideas. There is a short report of a fire in a block of flats and a child is found to be alone in a room. The report stops there, but your imagination carries on with the story. Why is the child alone? Have her parents locked her in while they go off to the pub? How did the fire start? Maybe the child and her mother live alone, having been abandoned by the child's father, or maybe the child was only left for a minute while the mother dashed out for something vital. Who found the child alone in the burning building? Was she badly burned or just frightened?

As you ask yourself these questions and decide on the answers, the plot begins to form. You become interested in your characters. The unknown child in the newspaper report takes on flesh and feelings, and when you begin to care what happens to her, you will find a satisfying ending to your story.

Get your plot idea from book titles. Read a selection and see what they suggest to you. Here are some in my bookcase: *Ride with Terror* by Henry Farrell. This makes me think of a story about a girl with a tearaway motor cycling boy-friend. *Breakdown* by John Boland. Could this be the story of a woman who longs for a baby and goes out and steals one? *The Shadow Wife* by Dorothy Eden. This suggests to me a tale of an apparently happily married couple who seem to have everything anybody could wish for in their comfortable life. Only the husband knows it is a sham. *What's Better than Money* by James Hadley Chase. A man with ambition puts his job before his wife and family. Jot down some of the titles of books on your shelves, and get to work on the plot ideas you receive from them.

Listening in to snippets of conversation on trains and buses is a fascinating occupation for any writer, and provides endless plot ideas. There's something about travelling that makes people want to chat. A woman sitting next to me recently on a plane trip to

Manchester confided in me that her daughter had left home six months previously to take a job in London. The girl wrote home often at first, then less frequently, and then not at all. In desperation the woman said she went to London and discovered her daughter was not known at the address she had given. I never heard what happened next because my journey ended, but I can make up my own ending. What would the girl's mother do next? To whom could she turn for help? And what made the girl lose touch with her home? Had she done something terrible, committed a crime, or innocently become involved in drug-peddling? Perhaps the girl got into debt or lost her job and disappeared because she hoped her mother wouldn't have to find out. There are endless possibilities to be found in this situation, and numerous stories about the girl and her mother could come out of it.

Find plot ideas in the problem pages of magazines. They can give you a host of stories. Study the problems and work out your own solutions. These may be quite different from those given by Marjorie Proops or Mary Grant. I read a letter recently that captured my imagination. The problem letter, purporting to have come from a girl of twenty, expressed the terrible fears of the writer who had been ill for some time and was terrified that she was never going to get well again. Neither the girl's parents nor her doctor had mentioned any specific disease and the girl was too scared to ask. It's easy to imagine how the girl was torturing herself, probably quite unnecessarily, and to write a story round the theme.

Many beginners find difficulty in deciding at what exact moment they should plunge into their story. The answer is quite simple. Begin your story at the beginning of the problem. This may seem obvious, yet it is good advice; begin by stating the problem round which your story is to be written. Finish off your tale when the problem has been satisfactorily solved. Tailor it lengthwise to suit your chosen market.

Characterisation

It is a sad fact that the best plot in the world will fail if your characters seem like puppets instead of real people. A story without characterisation sounds dull, rather like a newspaper report. For example:

At six-thirty a scarlet sports car stopped outside Number 44. A man jumped out, blew a kiss to the girl watching at the window, pulled a key from his pocket and let himself into the house. Ten minutes later Mr Jones, the owner of Number 44, arrived home unexpectedly in his secondhand saloon and parked it carefully behind the sports car.

That is reportage. You are not told much about the characters. You're vaguely interested to know who they all are, but reading that description doesn't make your heart beat any quicker, does it? You don't really care what's happening at Number 44 because the people don't come to life. Now let's look at the same passage with some characterisation added.

Jenny heard the roar of Julian's car long before it reached the house. She flew to the window, wincing at the noise. If only Julian's car had been less flamboyant. She was sure the neighbours would be watching from behind their curtained picture windows; watching and shaking their heads, clicking their tongues in disapproval because that Mrs Jones at Number 44 was having her boyfriend to see her again when her husband was away on business.

Jenny watched Julian jump out of his car, and a little hammering pulse began to beat in her throat when he looked up, smiled, and lifted his fingers to his mouth in a kiss. There was a pause, then the sound of his key in the lock. She wanted to rush out into the hall to greet him, but now that he was here, her legs refused to carry her across the room.

And then he was there. 'Hello Jenny,' he said softly, and with a little gulp, she flung herself into his arms.

Neither of them was aware of the minutes flying by. There was so much to say and afterwards, Jenny couldn't remember what had prompted her to glance through the window. Perhaps she'd heard the rumble of John's old car . . . but whatever caught her attention, she was totally unprepared for the sight of her husband's sturdy saloon as it pulled neatly into the kerb outside the house. Swinging round to face Julian, her fingers held to her mouth in an agony of indecision, she whispered: 'It's John. Whatever are we going to do?'

Now we have some substance to the scene. Seeing the events through Jenny's eyes makes us feel personally involved. Unlike the report, it's not just happening to some woman we don't know. Jenny is a real person with feelings and failings just like us. We've got some action into the story. Jenny flies across the room when she hears the car, Julian arrives noisily, rather brashly. He's a little insensitive. He doesn't care what the neighbours think. There is suspense and some mystery to keep your readers interested. Who is Julian? We know what the neighbours think, but they may be wrong. We know Jenny is agitated by his arrival, yet happy to see him. Then her husband arrives home unexpectedly. What's

87

going to happen next? We know a little about his character already. He drives a solid but unexciting car, and he parks it carefully. We can see already that he's quite different from Julian, can't we? And we're intrigued. We want to know what comes next and so we simply have to read on. It certainly looks as though Jenny is entertaining her boy-friend, but can we be sure? Maybe he's her spendthrift brother of whom her husband doesn't approve, and he can only come to see her when the husband is away. Perhaps he keeps asking her for money, and she gives him a loan without telling her husband. You have to decide who Jenny, John and Julian are and create believable characters your readers will want to know more about. Make your characters warm and likeable. If they act badly, show that they did it under stress or by mistake. It is human to be less than perfect and heart-warming to discover that other people, in fiction, are less than perfect too.

One easy and quick way to establish character is to do it through dialogue, i.e., the conversations your characters have between themselves. Let's take another example to explain what I mean. Here is a piece of dialogue that might come out of a short story.

'Mum! I can't find my see-through blouse anywhere and you promised to iron it for me. I've just got to wear it tonight and . . . oh! Hi Gran! Where's Mum?'

'Gone to her Guild meeting, Jane dear. It's Thursday, you know. Would you mind closing the door? There's such a draught and. . . .'

'But Gran! Mum promised . . . and there's nothing else I can possibly wear tonight at the disco . . . .'

'Isn't that it hanging behind the kitchen door, dear? Jane . . . don't forget to close the . . . oh dear, she's gone!'

Can you see how in just a few words of dialogue, you are given a clear picture of the three characters? Gran is patient, perhaps not too well because she feels the draught from the door. Jane is demanding, rather selfish because she's only concerned about her blouse, and she forgets to close the door. Mum is like most mums—ironing the see-through blouse before she goes out, making sure that Jane isn't disappointed.

Dialogue, more than any other single ingredient in a story, can paint instant pictures of the people you are writing about. As in the above example, make your dialogue suitable for the age and personality of your characters. Gran and Jane use different words and phrases in their conversation. Select the characters in your story with care. Get to know them, their habits, likes and appearances, just as you know your own family.

Take care when naming your characters, for an unsuitable name can give a wrong impression. Aunts and Mums may be called Brenda or Marjorie or Kath; John, David or Bill suggest that their owners are steady, reliable types. Give the children in your stories more unusual modern names . . . you'll find a selection in the births column of your local newspaper.

When working on your characters, remember that the distinguishing characteristics you give to them will determine how they will react in a given situation. For instance, a man may be brave on seeing a terrible car accident. He may offer his services and try to help. Another man seeing the accident may be a coward and run from the scene. The people in your stories must act in character if your reader is to believe in them.

Dialogue in your story
The words your characters use play a big part in

making your story appeal to your reader. Carefully handled dialogue is more attractive and easier to read than large paragraphs of descriptive narrative. My advice to a beginner is to present as much of the story as possible in dialogue form. Dialogue gives the reader instant information with the minimum of words; the personalities of your characters can be vividly portrayed by their conversation, as we have seen in the example of dialogue given in the previous paragraph on characterisation.

Let's look at an example of characterisation through clever dialogue. If you wanted to explain that Paul hated spending money, you could say simply: 'Paul was a mean man.' But how much more effective it would be if you made Paul betray his own character by making him say: 'Do we have to take a taxi? There's a bus-stop just down the road.'

Good dialogue must sound natural, but have you ever listened to natural dialogue? Put your tape recorder on the next time the family is gathered for a meal. Play it back when you are alone. You'll find the conversation terribly disjointed and difficult to follow. People hum and haw and take ages to get to the point of a story. This won't do in fiction where there is not sufficient space to include the irrelevances with which we pepper our normal conversation. In your stories, the dialogue must not *be* natural, it must merely *sound* natural. You use tricks to produce this effect.

First, make your sentences crisp and short for this helps to hurry the action of your story along. Break into people's sentences. In real life nobody talks for minutes at a time without someone butting in to make a comment or ask a question. If it is absolutely essential for long explanations to be given in dialogue, let another character break in with: 'Joe, get to the point. Did Elsie arrive home blind drunk last night?' Introducing another character's comments in this way will break up a long piece of dialogue and help to keep your reader interested in what is being said.

To help your reader readily to identify who is speaking, add the name of the person being addressed. For example: 'Hurry up with that ladder, Bill.'

On reading this piece of dialogue, the reader automatically realises that Bill's mate is speaking, and it is therefore unnecessary to add the speaker's name, i.e.: 'Hurry up with that ladder, Bill,' said Fred.

Don't forget, too, to slip in little gestures that make the character more vivid in the reader's mind. For example: 'She dismissed his excuse with a wave of her hand: "Don't lie to me, Stan".' The reader will accept that the words that follow the gesture must be made by the same person. These are both ways of avoiding using too many 'he saids' in your story.

Dialogue writing is a knack and one everybody can learn. Listen to the expressions people use and make a note of interesting ones. Eavesdrop when you're in a bus. At first, choose for your characters, people whose ways of speaking are well known to you. Unless you are Irish, don't have a Dublin bricklayer in your story. If you can't possibly do without him, then hover around a building site and listen. Radio plays can provide excellent examples of the use of dialogue. Listen regularly and note how the playwright uses his words.

And if you are writing for one of the currently popular teenage magazines, do not worry unnecessarily over your dialogue. Writers for these markets often feel that they don't know the modern phrases used by today's teenagers. I once felt uneasy on this point myself and was told by an editor of a 'young' magazine, that most of our young people speak fairly normal English, with just the occasional slang word popped in. As these do go out of fashion very quickly, and if you're not sure what's 'in'—leave them out. The editor can easily introduce one or two if he thinks they are essential to the story. Remember that slang and popular phrases soon date a story. Be especially careful not to put the phrases and sentiments that were popular when you were young into the mouths and minds of your modern teenage characters.

And when you've got your dialogue down onto paper, read it out aloud to yourself. Make sure it does one of the following three things:

1. Tells the reader the age, status and background of the person who is speaking.
2. Carries the story forward using easily understood words.
3. Shows the character of the speaker or explains how his mind works.

When checking through your dialogue, remember to erase sentences when your characters are just chatting, without performing one of the above essential functions of all dialogue.

Emotion

How to make your reader shake with laughter, tremble with fear, or swallow the lump in his throat.

It is important to realise that you may have thought up a super plot aimed at a particular woman's magazine, and produced good, recognisable characters and natural sounding dialogue, yet your story will fail to sell if the reader feels no emotion when reading it. The involvement of the reader is essential, and the best way to ensure that you've hooked his interest is to make your reader feel and suffer, fear and rejoice, along with your characters. You must make your reader care what

92

happens next to your characters, so that he will be quite unable to put the magazine down until your story is finished. Does that sound difficult? It is exactly what is achieved by the writer of any good short story and the secret behind his success.

If you have got to know your characters well, then you are halfway to ensuring that your reader will want to know them too. Have sympathy for the characters you create, remembering that if you don't, then your readers won't either. If you write your story with tongue in cheek, secretly thinking that your characters are making a big fuss about nothing, then your reader will sense this and instantly lose interest in your characters and what happens to them. You, the writer, must understand your characters' actions and motives, as though they were your own. You must feel sick at heart when the bottom drops out of your heroine's world. You must understand her distress to be able to write convincingly about it. If you don't achieve this rapport with the characters you have created, your story will never come to life.

Writing emotion into a story can be a little tricky at first. Too much and it ruins everything. It smacks of insincerity. Too little and the story is quite dead.

It is best for a beginner, therefore, to choose themes that interest him personally when attempting his first story for a woman's magazine. Pick a plot or theme that means something to you, a situation you or your family have experienced or a problem you recognise and about which you have strong feelings. If you are unsympathetic towards old people or children or alcoholics, then don't try to write about them unless you are sure you can do it without prejudice. Stick to the problems in your own life; if you are a harassed housewife with lovable but infuriating kids, then any domestic story

93

you write will bear the stamp of realism. Learn to write first about the things nearest to your heart, and later you will find that you can feel sympathy for other people with different problems.

Contrary to popular belief, the stories in women's magazines are not entirely escapist in content. They must bear the recognisable element of truth because even though the readers know they are reading fiction, they demand characters who behave in a realistic manner. There is no place for fantasy in these stories.

A common complaint from new writers is that they feel self-conscious about expressing feelings on paper. Perhaps they are afraid of revealing too much of themselves. We're all rather inclined to bottle things up inside ourselves. But as a successful short story writer, you learn to become sensitive to other people's feelings, and to convey this concern, through your writing, to your reader. Write from the heart and editors and your readers will love it.

Suspense

In every successful short story, there must be an element of suspense. Why do we read stories? Or novels? Or watch television plays? We get interested and involved with the characters, and we want to know what happens in the end. You, as the writer, must keep your reader wondering. If the reader knew the whole story, right from the beginning, then there would be no point in going on with it. Your reader may suspect that the tiff the two characters have over breakfast will be satisfactorily settled before the last word is read, but she must finish the story to discover how this is brought about. If the ending is made too clear at the beginning of a story, the suspense is gone and your reader will lose interest.

It is conflict, either physical or mental, that makes a story more gripping to your reader. Very often the appeal of a short story depends almost entirely on the conflict which, in some way or another, is brought into it. Don't we all feel sympathy for a character who is struggling against outside influences or his own impulses? This conflict may be between two people's will or between a man and his emotions, or a man and circumstances, so try to introduce one of these into every story you write.

Reader identification

This ingredient is vitally important in a women's magazine story. Fiction editors of these magazines believe that their readers unconsciously identify themselves with one of the characters in any story they read. Having done your market study, you will already know that the central character of most stories is a woman. Her age, status and inclinations will correspond to a great degree with those of the readers. The situations round which the stories are written will be similar to those experienced by the reader, her family and friends. Remember this point when deciding on the theme of your story. It is essential that you, as the writer, should hold a clear idea in your mind, of the type of reader you are aiming to please.

Endings

Finally, end your tale on a note of optimism. Make sure you have not left any loose ends, any character unaccounted for, or any puzzling happening unexplained. There is nothing more infuriating than to read a story and be left with the feeling that there are questions in your mind that the writer has failed to answer.

Sad endings are not very popular in women's

magazine fiction. If you can't achieve a happy one, then at least make it hopeful. Surprise endings, so beloved by readers of newspaper short stories, are not used in any great number in women's fiction.

When your story is nearing its end, don't drag it out so that your reader gets bored before the last paragraph. Finish off neatly, as crisply as you can, once your tale is told.

You're on the last lap now. You've worked out a neat, heart-warming plot, not too complicated, but strong enough to hold your reader's interest. Your characters are believable and very human, coping with their problems in a realistic way. You've introduced emotion. Your characters have shown fear or fright, pain or fulfilment. Now make sure you've got the right ending so that your reader will put down the magazine with a satisfied sigh, saying, 'That was good ... I liked it!'

Spend some time polishing your story; search for the right word, the telling last phrase or piece of dialogue to round off your tale. If the ending doesn't come easily to you, then put your story aside for a few days and begin another. When you dig it out and re-read it, you will come freshly to it, and be able to spot mistakes more easily. That difficult ending may suddenly seem easier to achieve.

The best ending of all is the one you achieve when an editor writes to say he is going to publish your story!

Rates of pay for women's magazine fiction vary widely, but on the whole, editors pay well for what they want. Fees of £3 to £50 per thousand words are currently being paid. Some magazines treat all their writers alike, while others pay special, higher rates when a writer becomes known to them. Several of the glossies pay highly for the work of well-known writers and offer less to the beginner. Nevertheless, if you can produce these stories, you will be paid well for your time and talent.

Markets for women's magazine stories

Any list of women's magazines that publish short stories would inevitably be out of date before this book reaches the bookshops. However, there are certain magazines that are well known and have been on the bookstalls for many years; some of these are listed below. Besides these giants there are innumerable small magazines which a writer must not neglect as they may represent a large slice of his daily bread and butter. Most of these are listed in the *Writers' and Artists' Year Book*. Keep an eye on your bookstalls for new publications as these are coming onto the market all the time.

In this chapter I have purposely omitted to mention the very popular type of women's magazines known as 'confession' or 'true-to-life'. This is a specialised market and is dealt with in the following chapter.

Woman	*Woman's Story*
Woman & Home	*Honey*
Homes and Gardens	*Woman's Weekly*
My Weekly	*Annabel*
Petticoat	*Woman's Journal*
Woman's Own	*Mother*
19	*Woman's Realm*
Good Housekeeping	

Note: The firm of D. C. Thomson of Dundee publishes many women's magazines such as *Red Letter, Red Star, Family Star* and others. This firm is especially sympathetic towards new writers, and frequently gives advice and helpful criticism.

Example of story sold to a women's magazine (*Annabel*)

QUICK, TELL ME THE WORST!

She was going home. Three weeks, two days and eighteen hours after being rushed away in an ambulance, here she was, sitting beside Mike in the car, with the hospital and her appendix operation safely behind her.

Laura felt almost her old self again, apart from rubbery knees and a faint dizziness that was probably due to excitement.

Mike looked fit and happy. And ultra-smart, Laura noted. His white shirt was crisply immaculate. For some odd reason Laura felt depressed at that. To lift her spirits, she began to ask about the girls.

'How are they? Did anything awful happen? I . . . I know you wouldn't tell me while I was in hospital, but now I'm strong enough to stand a shock. . . .'

Mike grinned. 'Nothing went wrong, Laura. Did you think we couldn't manage without you?'

'Of course not.' Laura bit her lip as Mike swung the car into their avenue.

'We were in good hands, anyway. I take back all I ever said about your sister Meg being too beautiful to be domesticated. She stepped in the night you were rushed off, and she's done wonders. She's kept the house shipshape, ironed my shirts and she's even persuaded Alison that it's not necessary to starve herself to a beanpole, to catch a boy's eye!'

'Really?' said Laura in a small, incredulous voice. *She* had been trying for six months to coax Alison to give up dieting.

'You'll be surprised when you see what Meg's done. For a career girl, she makes a great housewife.'

Laura managed to compose her face into a look of

98

admiration. Naturally she was pleased that everything had gone well in her absence. It was the first time she had left Mike and the girls to fend for themselves. She had not actually expected to come home to chaos and disaster. But neither had she imagined they would manage so beautifully without her.

Mike pulled up at the house.

'Welcome home, darling,' he said, kissing her. 'I've missed you.'

She would have believed him more if he had said that Meg's cooking gave him indigestion.

'Mum, you've lost weight!' seventeen-year-old Alison cried enviously, as she rushed out of the house. 'Don't bother with your things just now—I've got tea ready. Suzy will be down in a moment. She's having a bath.'

'A bath?' Laura murmured faintly, remembering her fourteen-year-old's aversion to tap water and tidiness.

Alison laughed. 'Don't look so stunned, Mum. Suzy's abandoned her hippy phase and now she's mad keen on the shining, scrubbed look. It's because Aunt Meg washes her hair twice a week and takes two baths a day.'

'I see.' Laura wondered why she herself had failed so miserably to influence Suzy.

'Oh, and Aunt Meg's been giving me lessons in flower arranging,' Alison was saying importantly. 'How do you like my creation on the hall table?'

'It's lovely,' Laura said absently as she stared round. All the paintwork had been washed. Everywhere was neat and shining and just as clean as if she had never been away. Cleaner, if anything. She let them push her into a chair without protest and took the cup of tea that Alison handed her.

'I made the almond tarts,' Alison boasted. 'Dad says they're just as good as yours. Do you like them?'

'Mmm, delicious!' Laura said. They were delicious but, somehow, they stuck in her throat. Then the door opened and in bounced Suzy. She flung her arms round Laura's neck.

'Mum, you're back! Are you sure you're better? Dad says you should have gone to Gran's for a week to convalesce. We would have been all right. We've managed fine without you, haven't we, Dad?'

'Very well,' Mike agreed, his face serious, but his eyes twinkling down at Laura.

Laura felt like throwing her cup at him. She restrained the impulse, drained the last, strangely bitter drop of tea, and smiled at the three of them. 'I'm so glad,' she said. 'Well, now you can all relax and I'll take over. I'll start with this washing-up.'

She saw the girls look at each other and begin to giggle. Mike grinned at her and took her arm. 'Come into the kitchen, dear,' he said. 'We—er—well, we've a little surprise for you.'

Laura suddenly felt much better. Why hadn't she thought of that before? Obviously they had been so busy tidying up the rest of the house that there hadn't been time to tackle the kitchen. Probably the sink was jammed with dirty dishes. Nobody would have remembered to clean the cooker or de-frost the fridge. Oh yes, she thought joyously. Now she would discover how they had missed her.

She halted in the kitchen doorway, gazing at the gleaming cooker, the dazzling pans and the empty sink. Her stomach did a slow somersault. Then she spotted the object on her stainless steel sink unit. It was squat and white, with a row of chromium knobs that seemed to be grinning maliciously at her.

'It's a dish-washer,' Mike announced proudly. 'It does the lot, from eggy spoons to sticky plates. Meg got me

100

to buy it. She said you'd find it a big help.'

'It's easy to work, Mum,' Alison assured her. 'I'll fetch the tea things. You'd like to have a go, wouldn't you?'

Laura glared at the gleaming monster with hatred in her heart. I'm redundant, she thought wildly. Nobody would have cared if I'd stayed away another month. I'm just not needed any more. Dredging up a feeble smile, Laura told her family:

'No, I won't try it out just now. I . . . I feel suddenly tired.'

They swept her sympathetically away, assuring her that she mustn't think of doing any housework for ages. They had everything under control.

Then the 'phone rang. Laura lifted the receiver and heard Meg's voice purring in her ear. 'Laura, are you better? I hope you found everything all right. Darling, I know I'm selfish, but you can't imagine how relieved I am to hand over to you.'

Laura sank into a chair. 'Really?'

'It's entirely your fault, Laura. I've just about killed myself trying to live up to your reputation. Mike's a pet, of course, but he needs at least four wives to look after him. As for the girls—I'd have exploded if I'd had to endure one more day of their wailing about how much better you do everything for them!'

Thoughtfully Laura replaced the receiver when Meg had finished. If what Meg said was true—or nearly true. Oh, but she probably said those things to make Laura feel that she had been missed.

The door opened and Suzy marched in, her arms full of school books.

'Mum, I don't want to bother you if you're feeling awful, but I've got the most ghastly homework. My German marks have been shocking since you went into hospital.'

101

Laura held her breath. 'Couldn't Aunt Meg help you?'

'Oh, Mum, she doesn't know German from double Dutch!'

Laura smiled. It was some consolation to know her absence had affected Suzy's German results.

Alison caught Laura in the hall, as she was following Suzy into the dining-room to help with the homework.

'Mum,' Alison whispered, her voice trembling with emotion, 'when you've helped Suzy, I want to talk to you. Privately, I mean. You see, Mum, there's this boy at the office and he keeps asking me out. I've been longing for you to come home so I could talk to you about it.'

Laura smiled as she watched Alison float upstairs, wrapped in her teenage daydreams that had to be shared with an understanding audience. Then Mike moved from the kitchen doorway and pulled her into his arms.

'You see how much we've all missed you,' he murmured into her hair. Laura began to laugh shakily, burying her nose in his jacket lapel. 'Oh Mike, stop pretending. You know you managed perfectly well without me. Everything's so tidy, you had plenty to eat and—and you didn't even get indigestion!' She blew her nose furiously to stop the tears from spilling over and added forlornly:

'After all, nobody's indispensable!'

'That's true,' Mike agreed, tipping up her face. Then he added softly, 'But you are irreplaceable.'

9 Writing the Confession Story

Beryl Sandwell

There is one large group of thriving women's magazines which I purposely omitted to mention in the chapter on women's magazine stories. These are known as the confession magazines. Almost every month new magazines appear on the bookstalls which publish first-person confession stories. There are now many magazines of this type, aimed at various age groups, and the signs are that the demand for such stories will increase in the next few years. For the writer able to produce this kind of story, there lies ahead a rosy financial future. More magazines of this type mean that more stories will be needed by editors, and this can only mean more cheques for the writers.

People are sometimes confused as to what a first-person confession story really is, but its name describes it exactly. It is a short story—usually between 2,000 and 8,000 words, with 4,000 words as the length most often used. It is written in the first person and purports to be the confession of the writer. Another popular name for these magazines is 'true magazines' and many people who never read them dismiss them as being sensational, but a careful study of them will reveal that this is rarely so.

The description 'true story' can be misleading, making some readers believe that the narrator has actually experienced the events around which the story is written, and that they are a record of actual happenings. The fact that the stories are all written in the first person adds to this feeling of reality, but a truer description would be that a confession story is 'true-to-life' with characters and a plot that are entirely believable.

It seems that for a story to be legally termed a 'confession' it must have a basis of truth although it is not necessarily something that has happened to you personally. Perhaps your story is written round a newspaper report or the incidents may have happened to people you know. In any case, the writer is allowed great latitude in his interpretation of the word 'confession'.

Now, for the beginner, longing to taste some success in the very lucrative short-story field, the confession magazines offer marvellous opportunities. If you pick up one of these magazines, and flip through it, you'll discover that they publish several short stories each month—six or more—and there are also some weekly confession magazines that use a similar number every week. The demand is enormous and this is one field of writing where the beginner has the same chance of success as the established writer. Because writers' names are not published, it is of no importance to the editor whose stories appear in his magazine. So you, as a beginner, will not have competition from well-known writers. The editor of a confession magazine simply buys a story she likes and which suits the editorial requirements of her magazine.

Moneywise, the confession story is very appealing. A minimum of £10 per thousand words is currently being paid, and as some stories run to 7,000 or 8,000 words, you will see that it is possible to earn a good income from this type of writing alone. A writer who sells exclusively and regularly to the confession markets can earn a very comfortable living for himself.

The popularity of these stories seems to stem from the fact that great care is taken to ensure that the backgrounds, characters and content of the stories are absolutely authentic. The readers must be able to identify themselves with the characters, and for this reason, the stories are about people who are not particularly beautiful, rich or clever. They are about ordinary people caught up in everyday problems, doing their best to find a way around them.

Although usually the 'confessor' or narrator, is female, and youngish, some of the stories are written from a man's or an older person's viewpoint. A crumbling marriage may be observed through the eyes of the mother-in-law who thinks the fact that she lives with the young couple is driving them apart. A man recently widowed, trying to cope with young children, his job and the household chores, may be the narrator of another story. If you think you can write with sympathy and sincerity, then try your hand at this specialised type of women's fiction.

Although, at first sight, these stories may seem simple, considerable skill is required to write to the required formula. Most of the action is carried in the dialogue, but in these stories, the action, though important, is secondary to the feelings of the narrator. As the story is being told in the first person, then her feelings, as the plot unfolds, become of prime importance.

Readers of confession magazine stories must have their interest captured as soon as possible once the story starts, which is why most of these tales begin with a dramatic opening. We join the narrator at a point in her life when some crisis or climax is being reached. For example, a young wife discovers she is pregnant one week after her husband has left her; a mother of three young children is told by her doctor that she must give up her job or injure her health, although she knows she must work to keep them; a middle-aged man sees his future in ruins when his firm declares him redundant at 45. In each of the above instances, the narrator has reached a point in life when drastic action and important decisions must be taken, and your reader wants to know what happens next.

As these stories are written as though being told by one person to another, simple words and easy, everyday phrases must be used. Long complicated explanations hold up the action, so keep your sentences short. Use the first 1000 or 1500 words of your story on the initial, dramatic opening, showing what problems face your narrator. The rest of the wordage will be used up in getting the narrator out of her predicament.

Almost any problem that people of today are facing can provide the story situation for your confession tale. It may deal with young or mature love, with unfaithfulness or jealousy, envy or tragedy. Your story could be a quiet, emotional tale or it could contain a lot of dramatic action. But whatever the problem you give your narrator, the characters must seem lifelike and the emotional appeal must be strong.

Despite the wide range of subjects that can be the basis of confession stories, the readers want to feel personally involved in the characters' problems. Your aim as the writer must be to make your story so vivid and inspiring that the reader can live through the events as though they were her own experiences. From your handling of the situation, your reader will receive help with her problems, or with the problems of someone she knows. You must try to throw some new, encouraging light on an impossible situation and show those of your readers who have lived through similar crises that others have had the same problems in life. Your story may warn readers that the result of certain mistakes can be tragic or unavoidable, or perhaps that life can offer a second chance after the most serious setbacks.

The basic requirements for a conventional women's magazine story and a confession story are the same, but the crisis that normally comes towards the end of a conventional story occurs at the start of a confession story.

After reading a number of confession stories, you will probably find out for yourself that most confession stories follow a similar pattern. The dramatic opening and crisis point is followed by a recap of events leading to this crisis. The narrator then makes a decision, acts upon it in the hope of improving her situation, and through her own efforts, finds a solution to her problem, or at least the prospect of improvement. This is a general guideline that applies to most confession stories, although there are some published which do not conform to the general pattern.

However, because many successful confession stories have a basic, recognisable shape, it is possible to write these stories following a certain formula and using a set of rules. They are rules that I personally believe that anyone can learn to follow. Start at rule number 1 and work your way steadily through the formula and when you have reached rule number 8, you will have mapped out the rough draft of your first confession story. Does this sound too easy? Don't imagine you'll be able to zip through the eight rules in a matter of minutes, because a lot of thought and imagination is required when you start using this formula. However, I can promise you that each time you use it, you'll find the going that little bit easier, and if you persevere you will eventually find that plot-building your confession story becomes second nature, and you will automatically apply the rules without realising you are working to a formula. So here we have the confession story formula, and in order to show you that it really works, we'll apply the rules later to a published confession story.

The confession-story formula

Rule 1. *Start with your main character, the narrator who is going to tell her own story.* It is not absolutely essential that she should be a woman, but a great number of these stories are written from the female viewpoint. Make your narrator a person whose life will be similar in many ways, to the lives of your readers . . . a housewife, a clerk or a shop assistant.

Rule 2. *Give your narrator a character weakness, flaw or attitude.* Make her lazy, bad-tempered, bitter, jealous, over-ambitious, slovenly, mean or dissatisfied with her life. She could be unfaithful, untrustworthy, a spendthrift or a bad cook.

Rule 3. *Place your narrator in a dramatic situation or crisis which has been brought about primarily by her character flaw.* For example, if you decide to have a character whose character flaw is that she's lazy and neglects her home, caring nothing for the comfort and well-being of her husband and children, then the crisis she brings upon herself may be that eventually her long-suffering husband decides he can stand her slovenly ways no longer and he leaves home, taking the children with him.

Rule 4. *Explain to your reader the cause of the narrator's*

108

character flaw. This is done in flashback once your narrator has reached the point of crisis in her life. The reason for this explanation is that your reader wants to like the narrator and feel sympathy for her, and we always feel more sympathetic towards someone if we know what triggered off her ill-temper, jealousy, etc. Another way to give your reader this information is to let your narrator tell the story herself in dialogue, to another character who is with her when she reaches the point of crisis in her life.

Rule 5. *The narrator's decision to act and the results she hopes to attain from such action.* This is the point where you start to resolve the problem and therefore bring your narrator through her crisis. So, the woman whose husband has left her because of her lazy ways has to decide how to get her husband and children back home again. She may not at first realise that she has driven him away. She may feel hurt or furious, guilty or aggrieved and her actions at this time will reflect these feelings.

Rule 6. *Unexpected result of narrator's action which makes her aware of her own character weakness.* The narrator's plans go awry. Things do not work out as she expects, and instead, she is made to realise the part she herself has played in bringing about the crisis in her life.

Rule 7. *Narrator endeavours to make amends.* She begins to think of others not simply of her own troubles. Her actions now reflect this new thoughtfulness.

Rule 8. *Narrator finds happiness or hope for better things in the future through her sincere attempts to atone for past mistakes*. This is where you reach your satisfactory ending. Your narrator now sees where she went wrong and that it isn't too late to change things by her own efforts. Some sacrifice on her part will be required so that your reader is satisfied that the narrator is now a better person, having learned her lesson the hard way.

In order that you may clearly see how the above confession formula can help you write your story, let's check the rules, one by one against a published story. Here is a brief synopsis of one of my stories which sold to a confession magazine.

THEN ANGELA CAME BACK

Joanna, jilted two years previously by Barry, when she was eighteen, has never recovered from the shock, never forgiven him or Angela the girl he went off with. Her bitterness has grown stronger with the years. In an effort to forget her unhappiness, she has thrown herself into her job and is now top stylist in a busy hairdressing salon, with hopes of owning her own salon in the near future.

Since Joanna's unfortunate experience and heartbreak, she has never been able to trust another man, not even Paul whom she met six months ago, and who refused to be discouraged when she told him she'd finished for ever with men and marriage.

'One of these days you'll stop feeling bitter about the past and when that happens I'll be around,' Paul told Joanna when she told him she wouldn't see him again.

One day when Joanna is working late at the salon, she discovers, to her horror, that the casual customer sitting in the chair in her cubicle is Angela, the girl

110

Barry married. As Joanna starts to set her hair, the atmosphere is icy and all Joanna's feelings of bitterness and anger come flooding back.

But Angela doesn't look very happy. She's shabby and tired-looking and while Joanna swallows down the words she always meant to say to Angela if ever they met, Angela begins to explain how Barry abandoned her when she became pregnant after three months of marriage, and that she now lives with her parents so that she can work to keep herself and her child.

Joanna listens numbly while Angela explains how remorseful she felt about taking Barry away from her. She adds that life hasn't been easy and that she has paid for the suffering she caused Joanna.

As Joanna hears Angela's halting explanations, her bitterness melts. Realising she has wasted two years of her life nursing hurt pride and mourning the loss of a man who was not worth a moment's thought, Joanna warms towards the girl she had previously hated. She works hard to make Angela look attractive with a new hair style when the girl admits she has a special date with a man who is going to marry her when her divorce frees her from Barry.

And when Angela leaves the salon, Joanna wishes her luck, and picking up the telephone tells Paul that she's put the past behind her, is missing him very much, and wants to see him again.

You will realise that the above is merely an outline of the confession story. The finished form of it ran to some 4,000 words, but the condensed form will suit our purpose. Now let's apply the confession story formula to this story.

Rule 1. *Start with your main character, the narrator who is going to tell her own story.* In our story, Joanna is the narrator and this is her story. We know her

111

problem and her thoughts on it and these must be explained in detail to the reader as the story progresses. Remember that if your reader is given a clear-cut picture of the way your narrator's mind is working, you achieve reader-identification from the start. Joanna is a hairdresser, young and unhappy . . . these points are made clear at the beginning.

Rule 2. *Give your narrator a character weakness, flaw or attitude.* Joanna's weakness is that she cannot forgive Barry and Angela, thinking they have destroyed her chances of happiness. She believes she'll never trust another man and therefore sends away Paul who obviously loves her.

Rule 3. *Place your narrator in a dramatic situation or crisis which has been brought about primarily by her character* flaw. The dramatic moment comes when Joanna confronts Angela at the salon. For years Joanna had hated this girl who stole Barry away from her. Having to do her hair and treat her politely as a customer is almost more than she can endure.

Rule 4. *Explain to your reader the cause of the narrator's character flaw. This can be done in dialogue or in flashback.* Now the reader must be told the whole background story leading up to the moment when Joanna finds Angela sitting in the chair in her cubicle. In my story I tell it through Joanna's thoughts as she begins to wash Angela's hair. In a series of little flashback scenes I show how Barry jilted Joanna a week before they were to marry. The reader hears how the arrangements had to be cancelled, the presents returned and how Joanna

112

had to take up the torn threads of her life, and face a very different future from the one she had planned. In another flashback scene I tell the reader how she finally met Paul but wouldn't let herself fall in love with him because of her unhappy experiences with Barry. At this stage in your story, your reader, while realising that Joanna is doing the wrong thing in sending Paul away, must also understand her motives and feel sympathy for the girl.

Rule 5. *The narrator's decision to act and the results she hopes to attain from such action.* Having refused to become involved with Paul, Joanna is convinced her only hope of satisfaction in the future must come from making a success of her career. That at least she can accomplish on her own without depending on anyone else. And so she works overtime in order to earn enough money to buy her own salon.

Rule 6. *Unexpected result of narrator's action which makes her aware of her own character weakness.* One night when she is working late and alone at the salon, Joanna is shocked and unnerved at having to deal with Angela, the girl she hates. But while having to listen to Angela's story, she learns of Barry's desertion and slowly realises she's been needlessly envying Angela. Instead of feeling bitter, Joanna realises what an escape she has had, how foolishly she has wasted the past two years. When Angela mentions her date with the man she hopes to marry, Joanna sees how brave the girl is in making a new start for herself and the baby. She wonders if her own failure to forget the

113

past has irretrievably ruined her chance of happiness with Paul.

Rule 7. *Narrator endeavours to make amends.* This is the point where Joanna forgives Angela for her part in the past tragedy. Her bitterness dissolves as she works on Angela's hair, making the girl look as attractive as possible for the evening's date.

Rule 8. *Narrator finds happiness or hope for better things in the future through her sincere attempts to atone for past mistakes.* When Joanna swallows her pride and telephones Paul, she is taking the first step towards a new and brighter future. Paul, we feel sure, will understand her change of heart. And the reader is left with a feeling of satisfaction because Joanna has stopped regretting the past and is ready to begin a new life.

I must mention here that although the majority of published confession stories adhere to a specific set of rules as given in the confession formula, there are others to be found which do not follow this pattern. However, as these require considerable skill, and know-how, I would suggest that the wise beginner will concentrate on producing the standard story and not concern herself with the exceptional story.

Try the confession story formula out on other published stories, and then use it to create your own, remembering that the way to achieve success is to write simply and sympathetically about people and their problems.

Write about your own life, your fears, hopes and frustrations. Transfer your thoughts to your characters—make them laugh and love, fear and fail—and your stories will sell, for editors are human too.

Finally, remember that these confession stories must

make your readers think. They provide points for discussion and argument. A friend of mine after reading a confession story told me seriously:

> I liked that story about the girl who hated her job but couldn't give it up because it paid well and she was up to her ears in debts that her husband didn't know about. If I'd been in her place, I don't think I'd have confessed to my husband, as that girl did. I'd have just kept quiet and stuck at the job until I'd paid off my debts. I just couldn't have faced my husband . . . .

My friend hadn't, I'm convinced, had a debt in her life. Nevertheless she had no difficulty in identifying with a woman in that situation. The writer of that story had succeeded in producing a realistic story with characters that were true-to-life.

Markets for confession stories

Buy and study magazines such as *True, Hers, True Story, Loving, Love Affair, True Romances*. Most magazines take stories from between 2,000 and 8,000 words in length, but between 3,000 and 6,000 is the length preferred by editors. Payment is always good and usually on acceptance, though it may vary according to quality and the editor's own evaluation. Recently an editor of a confession magazine told me that she is glad to pay £12 per thousand words for a story she likes. Other confession story magazines are *Truly Yours, Sincere Library* and *Woman's Story Magazine*.

10—Writing about your Hobby

Beryl Sandwell

In these days of increased leisure time and longer holidays, everybody has at least one hobby, so why not write about yours and get paid for it? Have you noticed the enormous number of specialised magazines on the bookstalls these days? Whether you collect stamps, veteran cars or Victorian jewellery, there will almost certainly be a magazine on the subject; if you decide to take up rose-growing, sailing or swimming there will be articles in newspapers and books to give you all the information you require.

Many people have more than one hobby, and you do not need to have specialised knowledge to write about it. On the contrary, your personal viewpoint and experiences as a novice will prove intensely interesting to a reader who is looking for tips. So long as you write simply and clearly about your pet pastime, people will read with interest and editors will ask you for more.

If amateur acting is your hobby, then write up an account of your feelings the first time you were on stage. Do it humorously if possible, for this will help to sell your piece. What about the first garden you tried to make out of the tip the builders left behind? If it nearly broke your heart, write about that too. Send it off to one of the popular gardening magazines, and wait for the cheque to arrive!

A glance through the magazine catering for your

particular hobby will give you an idea of the length of article published. Reading the letter page can sometimes provide you with an idea for an article. Remember always to check facts before including them in your piece, and don't be put off by the thought that anything you could write has probably been read often before. It may be true, but remember that it is your viewpoint, your personal and unique approach to the subject that your reader wants to hear. A friend of mine, interested in gardening, told me some time ago of her successes and failures with plants she brought to the Isle of Man from her previous home in the south of England. I told her to write up her experiences in a series of articles on 'Making a Manx Garden'. This she did, and up to date has sold four of them to a gardening magazine.

Besides your own hobbies, why not write about those of your family? If you are a golf widow, instead of moping at home in your husband's absence, make your thoughts on the subject earn cash for you. Children work their way through half a dozen hobbies while they're at school and your efforts to cope with their various enthusiasms will be read avidly by other mums.

Maybe, like me, you're married to a car-touring enthusiast who insists on driving thousands of miles each holiday. If so, remember, next time you go, to jot down anecdotes of the people you meet and the interesting and unusual sights you see, and when you get home again, write them up. There are numerous motoring magazines that use articles on touring in this country and abroad. Photographs to illustrate your article will add appeal to your piece and you will get paid for those too, if the editor uses them. Quarter or half plate prints are generally needed for reproduction, with a sharp, glossy finish.

In Britain we are a nation of pet-lovers, so why not write about yours or those of your family. Remember that specialist knowledge is not necessarily required. I remember the day I found myself mum-in-charge of a tortoise for the first time in my life. Knowing absolutely nothing about tortoise hates and habits, I sat down to write a cry for help in the form of a 400 word article which I sent off post haste to a pet paper. By return came the editor's cheque and the request that I should send him any other amusing stories I'd got on pet-keeping. His letter was followed almost immediately by a flood of helpful letters from experienced tortoise owners who were eager to educate me and tell me all they knew.

As we are incurable animal lovers in our family, I soon had the material to write other experiences about keeping rabbits, siamese cats and budgies. You see the idea? Write about the everyday problems that crop up connected with your spare-time activities, and you'll find they will sell.

When you have dealt with the purely practical aspects of your hobby, then go to your library and look up the history of it. Some encyclopaedias give a concise history of hobbies. When was knitting invented, and who by? What were the first knitting needles made of? Who made the first knitting machine? Think about your hobby, and look up the answers to questions about it. Articles about the origin of your hobby and about famous people connected with it will find a ready market, and you can discover all the information you need from a visit to your local library.

If your hobby is an unusual one, if you collect priceless china houses or Italian figurines, then your local newspaper might well be interested in an article about you and your collection. Is there a glossy, county magazine that covers the area in which you live? Tell them about your hobby too. You will probably find that the articles published in, for example, *Yorkshire Life* run to 1500 words or even longer.

If your knowledge about your hobby is extensive, then of course you will have the qualifications to write seriously and informatively on the subject. Don't keep this knowledge to yourself, but give others the benefit of your experience, by producing articles crammed with up-to-date information. Send them off to the specialist magazine covering your hobby. You never know, you may end up writing a regular column for the editor on your pet subject!

Don't forget when you've written your article for your hobby magazine, the information in it may be written up again and used in a piece to suit a more general readership. Several 'general' magazines like *Weekend* or *Saturday Titbits* print paragraphs about people's unusual and interesting hobbies.

Have you ever thought about writing a book about your particular interest? If you have been collecting cigarette cards or Edwardian silver pepper pots all your life, you have probably acquired sufficient information and know-how to fill a book. Think how 'collecting-mad' some people have become over the past few years. It was once almost impossible to buy a book about any hobby unless you were prepared to invest in some outdated tome that would cost you pounds. Nowadays bookshop shelves are full of paperbacks covering most hobbies and pastimes. If your particular hobby is a little out of the ordinary, you may find that nobody has written a recent book on it. If this is the case, go ahead. Write a book for the keen collector, another for the amateur who is thinking of taking up a new hobby and after that, what about a book on the subject written specially for children?

When your book is written, you will have to find a publisher for it. Lists of publishers and the types of books they specialise in can be found in the *Writers' and Artists' Year Book*.

So don't just enjoy your hobby. Write about it and let it earn some cash for you.

General tips on writing about your hobby

1. Study all the magazines on the market that deal with your particular hobby. Note the length of the articles used, the amount of technical information given and the subjects covered.
2. Keep your articles short and interesting, remembering that readers soon become bored with long, involved descriptions and rambling explanations. The most popular length is 1000 words or less.
3. Read the articles the editor has already published and paid for and decide whether he wants the material written up in such a way as to amuse, instruct or interest readers of his magazine.
4. Remember to check important facts before including them in your article. It is easy for little mistakes to creep in. Just think of the disastrous outcome if you inadvertently gave wrong measurements and incorrect amounts of ingredients, e.g. inches of material instead of yards, and a pound of salt instead of a pinch!

Rates of pay vary widely according to the circulation of the magazine. Some editors pay between £5 to £15 per thousand words, though a well-researched article may command up to £50.

Some magazines catering for hobbies

Aeromodeller　　　　　　*Popular Gardening*
British Chess Magazine　　*Animals Magazine*

Climber and Rambler	*Cage and Aviary Birds*
Canoeing Magazine	*Antique Collector*
Gems	*Philately*
Gold Illustrated	*Coins*
Popular Camping	*Do-It-Yourself*
Skier	*Good Motoring*
Small Boat	*Photography*
World Bowls	*Embroidery*
Yachting Monthly	*Homes and Gardens*

A full list of hobby markets can be found in the *Writers' and Artists' Year Book* and *Willing's Press Guide*.

Sports writing

If your only hobby happens to be following a particular sport, there are two ways in which you can earn cash while indulging in your favourite pastime. Thousands of men and women regularly attend sports gatherings, as players or fans. If you are one of these, don't overlook the opportunity to make money from sports reporting. Most local papers will pay for a report of a local amateur game of any description; the amount you can expect will depend on the number of lines used in the paper for your piece plus any out-of-pocket expenses such as bus fares, telephone calls etc.

Another profitable side of sports writing is the compiling of letters about sports matters for various magazine and newspaper columns. These include the *Sunday Sun, New Reveille,* the *Daily Mirror, Weekly News,* and the *Sunday Mirror.*

If you consider that you know enough about your favourite sport to produce a workmanlike report, then make yourself known in the first instance to your local newspaper's sports editor. Tell him of your interest and submit a sample report so that he can judge for himself whether your knowledge of the game is adequate. If you are a really keen player or spectator, the chances are that your local sports editor will be interested and you will probably be taken on as a freelance sports correspondent. After this, you may expect to be asked to attend one match a week. The normal procedure is for you to telephone in a short report of about 50 words at half time, giving the scorers of goals if it is a soccer match, including a few interesting remarks on the game so far. Alternatively, you may simply be asked to telephone in the half-time score. After the final whistle, you will be asked to write anything from 75 to 150 words on the whole game. This may have to be telephoned in to the copy desk at a specific time, and in that case will be dictated by you to the copytaker. As in all reporting, names must be checked carefully.

You will realise that sports writing can be very interesting and rewarding, especially if you can use your local knowledge of players and teams to add colour to your reports. Always be on the look out for news items about officials and sportsmen or women which you may be able to write up later into articles for the gossip pages. You could earn yourself several cheques from the one assignment.

Letters on your favourite sport
Many daily newspapers and general magazines carry opinion columns covering sporting matters from football to fishing. The compiler of such a column publishes letters received from members of the public commenting on any aspect of sport. You do not need to be an expert to write convincingly and interestingly; a glance at these columns will show you that many letters come from television armchair spectators. Most of us have felt like dashing off such letters after perhaps watching sport on television. In the days when Brian Clough was

at Middlesbrough, the following letter earned £3 in a newspaper sports column:

Surely any player, including Brian Clough, can decide to have a change of employer. This situation occurs every week in smaller clubs and it is settled as a domestic matter and not headlined.

As it was, certain sections of the press blew this situation up out of all proportion, hurting the Middlesbrough team, management and supporters. I am glad Brian and his Merry Men answered these press critics by going nap against Bristol Rovers.

As soccer is my own favourite sport, I'm always on the look-out for subjects that may interest football fans, and the *Sunday People* sports section printed the following recently as their Letter of the Week with an award of £5.25.

Newcastle especially, and all clubs, will have to do something practical about crowd hooliganism and pitch invasions before the start of next season. One way to stop this, apart from erecting unsightly high wire netting around the ground, is to pen the whole of the standing room. The pens could be numbered and limited and season tickets could be issued. The pens would prevent swaying and wholesale movement of large crowds, and assist the police to get the trouble-makers cleared down the gangways. Let us hope the Clubs will do something about it this summer.

Emergency situations are always with us and can often provide the keen-eyed sports writer with subject matter. The restriction on the use of power when the miners were on strike inspired this letter:

Having been an advocate of Sunday soccer for years, I have been pleased to see that thousands of sportsmen in this country have turned out during the last few Sundays to watch Cup and League games. What a godsend for the struggling Third and Fourth Division Clubs! Now that Sunday games have started, they should continue when the present emergency ends. If the authorities decide to revert to Saturday and weekday only soccer, they deserve all the club bankruptcies they will get.

If they are worried by the religious aspect of Sunday soccer and its possible interference with church-goers, why don't local churches and clubs combine to have a service either before the match starts or during a longer interval when a collection could be taken?

There are no doubt numerous points on which you, as a spectator of sportsmen, feel strongly. A few words written briefly to a sports column editor will air your grumble and probably bring you a cheque. The constant rise in the cost of entry to sports grounds or the poor play in many matches could be your complaints as well as mine. For example:

Like everything else, the cost of watching soccer matches is increasing. I think the time has come for the game's administrators to ensure that the spectator gets his moneysworth.

Far too much time-wasting goes on; players pretending to be injured ... continually kicking the ball into touch ... and taking their time in dead-ball situations just to waste another few seconds. Why not kill all time-wasting stone dead by installing time clocks, as used in ice hockey games, in all grounds?

125

When the ball is not in play, the clock stops, and only starts again when play commences. This would at least ensure that spectators saw 90 minutes' play.

Although the foregoing examples of writing about your favourite sport apply to soccer, you can write about your own sport in exactly the same way. Even if you never enter a sports-ground and are simply a television spectator, your opinions and ideas about the game are valuable and of interest to fellow viewers, so keep an eye open for opportunities to air your ideas and earn cash from them. Besides national and local newspapers, many local sporting pink and green newspapers have their own columns for sporting letters. Some offer cash and others prizes. Others give tickets for games fixtures.

Examples of articles written about a favourite pastime or interest

TOWN BIRD

Although house-sparrows and starlings are considered to be our commonest city-dwellers, during the winter months, thousands of seagulls also flock into towns. In almost every locality, coastal, rural or industrial, at least one of the gull species regularly frequents the inland stretches of water. On park lakes, canals and rivers, they swoop and dive for food, apparently finding it more plentiful in these places in winter, than in the seas around the coast.

The black-headed gull is generally the one seen parading in city parks, squabbling over the remains of packed lunches and the contents of litter bins. It is often mistaken for the common gull, as its distinctive black head loses most of its blackness in winter when its plumage is mainly grey and white. As soon as the

126

brighter days arrive, the black-headed gull deserts the city, and heads for a nesting place far removed from people and traffic. In their thousands, they congregate in deserted marshy stretches of moorland, miles away from roads or houses; in the peaty heather they lay their large grey-green eggs in flimsy nests roughly made of dried stalks and grasses.

The common gull with its yellow beak and pure white plumage is larger than the black-headed gull, and rarely visits stretches of inland water or cities. It breeds in remote spots on the Irish and Scottish coasts; the young gull can be distinguished by a black band across its tail feathers which disappears when the bird is fully mature.

Seaside visitors are familiar with the gull seen more frequently in this country than any other of the species. This is the herring gull. It is a very large, handsome bird, with huge wings, pale grey back and white underparts. Its beak is bright yellow with a blob of bright orange in the lower mandible. It is usually seen perching on chimney pots and roofs, diving to accept bread from a holidaymaker's outstretched hand or strutting proudly up and down the promenade. It fixes friend and foe alike with a beady, vicious glare and screeches a raucous protest when displeased. When fully grown, it looks immaculate, but during the first few years of its life when its plumage is a mottled brown colour it presents a less striking appearance. The herring gull rarely strays more than a few miles inland, even in the stormiest weather, preferring to scavenge on the beaches or accept food from winter residents.

THE DISAPPEARING MANX CAT

Over the past few months, owners of tail-less cats in the Isle of Man have been keeping a watchful eye on their pets. A local newspaper reported that cat-stealers have been operating in the Isle of Man, and several cats have been stolen.

Although cats without tails were fairly common in the British Isles before the last war, they are now quite rare, even in their native island home. A few years ago, a census of the Manx cat population revealed the alarming fact that there were only a few hundred true Manx cats in the Isle of Man.

An experimental cat centre was set up under the Board of Agriculture to breed Manx cats. Despite this governmental action, however, tail-less cats are still rare, one of the reasons for this being that it is difficult to breed true Manx. If two Manx cats are mated, they will produce kittens with normal tails, kittens with half-tails or stumps or kittens without tails. Continual breeding of Manx to Manx seems to produce a lethal factor with the kittens dying just before or soon after birth.

The tail-less cat, or Rumpy as it is called, must be quite definitely without any vestige of a tail. A true Manx cat has a hollow at the end of its backbone where a normal cat's tail begins. To discover if the cat is truly tail-less, it should be possible to place the end of the thumb into the recess or hollow at the end of the backbone. The vertebrae should end there. High back legs give the Manx cat a rabbity gait—more of a hop than a walk. They should have a double coat, the top one being soft and open with a very thick undercoat. They can be any colour, but the head should be large with broad, high cheekbones and a nose slightly longer than that of the normal short-haired cat. Ears should be wide at the base and pointed at the tips. They make very intelligent pets, although they are difficult to rear.

Manx cats are extremely popular in America and

throughout the world, and it has become impossible to keep up with the demand for Manx kittens.

One famous Manx cat to leave the Cattery was Peta, who was presented to the Home Office in 1964 by the Manx Government, and as a permanent member of the staff there—Home Office Mouser—she received a weekly wage of 25p.

There are many legends surrounding the origin of the Manx cat, but the Government veterinary surgeon who supervises the Manx Cattery thinks that the tail-less cat is a mutation of the common short-haired British cat which occurred two or three hundred years ago in the Isle of Man.

11—Writing Competition Slogans

Jon Atkinson

You may think at first that entering prize competitions has absolutely nothing to do with writing. As some of the hundreds of regular contestants will no doubt agree, competitions are great fun, and if you are clever with words, your chances of winning are very much enhanced. I am not referring here to crosswords and newspaper contests where a money fee is charged for entries, but to the trade contests in which the entrant has to complete a puzzle and add a slogan. This consumer contest is really a device to promote sales of a particular product and invariably one of the competition conditions is that labels, box ends or some other proof of purchase must accompany each entry.

The total prize money varies in competitions of this kind; you may win £1000 or a new car or colour television set, a holiday in America or a year's supply of tinned fruit. You will have read of syndicates formed by housewives who try to win many prizes with their many attempts. There is no doubt that chance plays a big part in consumer contest wins, and the housewife competing on her own may achieve success with one attempt. I can vouch for this from personal experience. I have sent in over a hundred attempts in a coffee competition and won nothing; on several other occasions, I've won a substantial prize from a single entry.

The usual trade competition asks for a number of

characteristics to be placed in order of merit, and when you realise that up to 300,000 entries may be received for one competition, it also follows that hundreds of competitors will get the order correct. However, in most contests of this type, it is the slogan asked for which will decide the winners. Slogans are the money-spinners of consumer contests and consequently many journalists and writers with a knowledge of words and their meanings are able to produce first-class winning slogans.

It is interesting to think that many of today's familiar slogans now in everyday use were thought up by advertising copy-writers or competition slogan addicts at one time or another. Here are a few of the best known:

Drinka Pinta Milka Day (National Milk Publicity Council)
Beanz Means Heinz (Heinz Baked Beans)
Go to work on an egg (Egg Marketing Board)
High speed gas puts you in control (British Gas)

In consumer contests, it is usually the well-thought out, eye-catching phrase or slogan that decides the outcome of the competition. And although most of us enter, hoping to win the major prize, there are also hundreds of smaller prizes well worth having.

Organising yourself to compete
Organisation is essential if you aim to be a successful regular competitor. Make a start by collecting competition forms from supermarkets, shops and stores; encourage your family and friends to watch out for them too. It is also a good idea to save all the labels from cans used in the home. I have a large plastic bag

pinned under the kitchen table and all can labels are automatically removed and placed in the bag. Once a week or so, when the bag gets full, I empty it, group the labels into bundles fastened with elastic bands, and store them in an old suitcase, so that when a competition is announced by a particular product, ten-to-one I have some labels ready for enclosure with my entry.

The competition entry forms are placed separately in envelopes on which I mark, in pencil, the closing date and name of the competition. These pencil details can be erased later when the competition entry form is completed and I am ready to send it off. All contest envelopes are kept together in closing date order to make sure I send them off in good time.

It is a good idea to keep a competition book in which to record the contests entered, number and types of prizes, date sent, date of result, name of competition, and, if you are successful, the prize you receive. A record of all the slogans you invent should also be kept just in case yours don't win a prize, and therefore may be used again some time.

Writing a slogan
When writing a slogan, first carefully read all that the firm has to say about the particular product associated with the contest. You will find plenty of material on the label, packet or tin and also in advertisements. These all give you clues as to what the organisers want you to say about their product in your slogan. Allow yourself plenty of time to think about your slogan. Try not to leave it until the last few days before the competition closing date, as this may result in a quickly contrived effort or the sort of phrase or jingle that is obvious and will undoubtedly have sprung to the minds of hundreds of other competitors.

Sketch out your rough ideas; twist phrases around in your mind, let them simmer for a while. The fewer words you include in your slogan, the better it will sound. Remember the famous ones that are now household phrases, like 'Guinness is Good for You' and 'Players Please'. Make your words mean something important about the product, and if they roll smoothly off the tongue as well, like the two examples given above, you will stand a better chance of winning. With practice you will find that catchy phrases spring more easily to your mind. Strive for originality. Simple, straightforward slogans usually have more impact than flowery, insincere phrases. Don't make exaggerated claims about the product. Sometimes a slogan in verse is requested, but it is best to steer clear of rhyming jingles unless the competition rules ask for this type of slogan.

Study the rules of the competition and remember that failure to comply with them will automatically result in your entry being rejected.

Sending in several entries to one particular competition is an excellent idea so long as you have some good slogans worked out for each submission.

Don't forget to enclose the box tops, labels, etc., which have to accompany your entry form. Fasten these firmly to each other but do not attach to your entry form. This is to prevent accidental damage to your competition form when your entry is being examined; labels attached by a pin or clip may be roughly torn off and your chance of success ruined before it reaches the judges.

Once your entry has been despatched, forget it, and turn your mind to the next competition. It will then be even more of a surprise when the postman brings a prize, for one of the joys of being a regular competition addict is the constant knock on the door and the arrival of odd-shaped parcels. The day is never humdrum or dull when it may bring news of yet another competition win. Notification of success comes in various ways, by letter, telegram or personal call; in a list of winners published in a trade journal or simply by the arrival on the doorstep of another exciting, unexpected parcel.

There are many housewives who are successful prize-winners and have become expert in the competition field. You can spend as much or as little time as you can spare on this particular way of writing for cash awards or prizes in kind. Certainly your chance of success is high if my experience is anything to go by. Throughout the years I have won a constant stream of prizes, from holidays abroad to hats, food and picnic hampers galore, tea and dinner sets, cameras, kettles, carpet sweepers, rugs, and, of course, cash prizes.

If you have children, encourage them to enter competitions too. It makes them think, and teaches them that they can't win the big prize every time.

For competition addicts the regular purchase of the *Competitors' Journal* is essential, for it lists almost every competition that is launched and at the same time has its own monthly short story competition on a given subject. If you are looking for helpful tips from an expert in the competition game, a paperback called *Win Prize Competitions,* written by Robert Kendal, will convince you that here is a worthwhile pastime at which you can become expert. Others are doing it every day. So why not you?

Make a start today by pinning a large plastic bag under your kitchen table to hold labels, and look out for the competition entry forms on your next shopping trip. Remember the successful competition winner's slogan: 'If you're not in, you can't win!'

In conclusion

Having read through the foregoing chapters in which we set out to describe specific ways in which cash can be earned from writing, we trust our readers will be stimulated and encouraged to try their hand. We have purposely picked out avenues of opportunity for the would-be successful writer in which we consider the chances of achievement are the most promising. We have written frankly about how we write and aim for specific markets. We have not touched upon the hundred and one other ways there may be to earn cash from writing: we have simply stuck to those in which we ourselves have had some success.

Writing can be a career or a pleasant pastime, depending on the time and effort involved. From it can be derived considerable material benefit, and also great personal pleasure and satisfaction. It is a field in which men may compete with women and young with old, where the pensioner shares the same opportunity as the rising young executive. Age is no barrier; we know of successful writers who took up the craft on retirement, and school children who earn regular pocket money with their letters to magazines.

If you become a writer, your life will never be dull. The arrival of the postman becomes the highspot of the day, and even an enforced stay indoors recuperating after flu may be welcomed because it provides you with extra time for writing.

Money earned by the pen or typewriter seems to be worth far more than its face value. Even small awards provide spectacular encouragement to the beginner. You may have heard writers declare that they enjoy the craft of writing, and are not concerned whether their work sells or not.

Whilst agreeing wholeheartedly that there is immense

136

satisfaction in producing any kind of creative work, we also believe that acceptance and payment is the only proof that our work is up to publication standard. Families and friends may tell us they like and enjoy reading what we write. But when some strange editor we have never met decides that he likes and enjoys reading our work too, then this is true success.

May we wish you happy, successful writing, and an abundance of our favourite type of letter which begins:

Dear Sir or Madam,
We hope to publish your piece in a forthcoming edition of our magazine and look forward to hearing that a fee of ten pounds per thousand words is acceptable to you . . .

Index

Book publishers, 121
Books and magazines for writers, 11-12, 17, 31, 44, 135

Characterisation, 86-89
Contributors' Bulletin, 12
Competitions, 131-135
    entry forms, 133-134
    how to win, 131-135
    prizes and rewards, 131
    slogans, 133-134
Competitors' Journal, 135
Confession magazine stories, 97, 103-115
    example, 110-111
    formula, 107-110, 111-114
    markets, 115
Contributors' Bulletin, 12

Dialogue, 89-92

Emotion, 92-94

Fillers, 13-18
    markets, 16-18

Gossip columns, writing for, 33-39

Hobbies, writing about, 117-129
    examples, 126-129
    markets, 121-122

Income tax, 11

Keeping records, 9-10, 28, 133

Market study, 35, 77-81

Photographs, 118
Plots, 83-86, 93
    from book titles, 84
Presentation, 9, 10-11, 15, 23-24, 25-26, 58-59
Problem page letters, 85

Radio, writing for, 65-76
    BBC Morning Story, 69
    commercial, 71
    example script, 72-76
    local, 66, 69
    short story, 65-66, 69
    talks, 65-69
Reader identification, 95
Reader's Digest, 17

Readers' letters, 19-30
  children's, 27-28
  examples, 24-26
  markets, 30-31
  on a set subject, 28-29
  seasonal, 29

Story endings, 95-96
Suspense, 94-95
Sports, writing about, 122-126
  letters, 123-126

Titles, 58-59, 67
Tools for the writer, 9-10
Trade press, writing for, 41-52
  American, 48-49
  examples, 49-50, 50-51
  information sheets, 44-45
  markets, 51-52

Typing lessons, 9
Typing paper, 10

Willing's Press Guide, 16, 31, 44
Women's magazine stories, 14, 77-102
  example, 98-102
  ingredients, 79-96
  markets, 97
Women's page, writing for, 53-64
  examples, 59-64
  subjects, 53-59
Writers' and Artists' Year Book, 16, 31, 44, 72, 97, 122
Writers' circles and clubs, 12
Writers' notebooks, 9-10, 57, 83